# Storytime

## Easy storytelling techniques for parents, teachers and carers

### R.M. COLE

HAY HOUSE

Australia • Canada • Hong Kong • India
South Africa • United Kingdom • United States

**First Published and distributed in the United Kingdom by:**
Hay House UK Ltd, 292B Kensal Rd, London W10 5BE.
Tel.: (44) 20 8962 1230; Fax: (44) 20 8962 1239. www.hayhouse.co.uk

**Published and distributed in the United States of America by:**
Hay House, Inc., PO Box 5100, Carlsbad, CA 92018-5100. Tel.: (1) 760 431 7695 or
(800) 654 5126; Fax: (1) 760 431 6948 or (800) 650 5115. www.hayhouse.com

**Published and distributed in Australia by:**
Hay House Australia Ltd, 18/36 Ralph St, Alexandria NSW 2015.
Tel.: (61) 2 9669 4299; Fax: (61) 2 9669 4144. www.hayhouse.com.au

**Published and distributed in the Republic of South Africa by:**
Hay House SA (Pty), Ltd, PO Box 990, Witkoppen 2068.
Tel./Fax: (27) 11 467 8904. www.hayhouse.co.za

**Published and distributed in India by:**
Hay House Publishers India, Muskaan Complex,
Plot No.3, B-2, Vasant Kunj, New Delhi – 110 070.
Tel.: (91) 11 4176 1620; Fax: (91) 11 4176 1630. www.hayhouse.co.in

**Distributed in Canada by:**
Raincoast, 9050 Shaughnessy St, Vancouver, BC V6P 6E5.
Tel.: (1) 604 323 7100; Fax: (1) 604 323 2600.

Copyright © Ronny M. Cole, 2008, 2010

The moral rights of the author have been asserted.

The author of this book does not dispense medical advice or prescribe the use of
any technique as a form of treatment for physical or medical problems without the
advice of a physician, either directly or indirectly. The intent of the author is only
to offer information of a general nature to help you in your quest for emotional
and spiritual wellbeing. In the event you use any of the information in this book
for yourself, which is your constitutional right, the author and the publisher
assume no responsibility for your actions.

A catalogue record for this book is available from the British Library.

ISBN 978-1-8485-02147

Printed and bound in Great Britain by CPI Bookmarque, Croydon, CR0 4TD.

# Storytime

These stories are for

_____

They were created in a spirit of love by

_____

Date:_____

This book is dedicated to Adam and Arielle.

Top commendations go to Tooty the Train, and special thanks to Hampy, who saved the day too many times to count.

Deryn, thank you for Believing in me.
USDBQM.

# Contents

# Foreword

We had just returned from a wonderful but hectic holiday. The whole day had been spent travelling. We were really tired. When we got home, the children had a sudden burst of energy; I had a renewed burst of exhaustion. They wanted a story! I started looking for a book to read to them. No, they wanted me to make up a story. I was having difficulty in remembering my name! How was I going to make up a story?

I told them to get ready for bed and I would think of something. I felt that would give me some breathing space to come up with a storyline. I was wrong. All bright-eyed, washed and in their night-clothes, they were ready. I was totally blank.

Pretending that I was ready, I told them to snuggle down for their story. I glanced up at the chest of drawers and noticed the night-light. It was in the form of a little train with a 4-watt bulb inside. Suddenly my brain came back to life. I had an idea. I found myself speaking: 'One day, Tooty the Train was huffing and puffing along the tracks. He was very small for a train. In fact, he was so small, you almost couldn't see him. He was inspecting the tracks for loose spikes, when all of a sudden he heard a strange sound. Down from the sky came a big spaceship. It landed right on a nearby switch-track. The door of the spaceship began to open. Tooty was frozen in his tracks – literally. He watched as two alien creatures began to leave the ship. They each had three eyes. They looked around and spotted Tooty. The first one began to wave, but lost his balance on the tracks and fell face-down on the ground. The other alien looked quite embarrassed. They walked over and explained that they needed help. Tooty introduced himself and ...'

The story concluded with Tooty flying off in their ship and helping them on a far-off planet. There was a problem with their trains, and they had come in search of someone who could help. Somehow they had heard about Tooty. He ended up back in his little bed in the roundhouse that night.

The children loved this story. I was a resounding success. The next night they asked for another 'Tooty'. I did not realize it then, but that was the first of about 3,000 stories I would tell them about Tooty and a host of friends he met in his strange travels.

From time to time I would weave little pieces of wisdom and moral content along the way. As my children got older, they grew more sophisticated and began to realize that many of the things Tooty and his friends did were impossible. They didn't mind, but it gave us the opportunity to explore the nature of our universe. Of course, science doesn't know everything yet, but there's certainly plenty to learn about. And so we learned together.

In speaking with other parents, I discovered that very few made up stories for their children. They read to them instead. I think that's great. I strongly recommend reading books to children. However, I also believe we can achieve more. We can create our own legacies with our children.

I wanted to share my experience with others, and so this book was born. It includes information that goes beyond the art of simply relating creative stories. My belief is that we can use bedtime stories to guide our children into being happier and more productive.

My desire is for my readers to share high-quality time with their children.

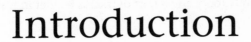

# Introduction

# Introduction

Making the decision to have a child is momentous – it is
to decide forever to have your heart go walking around
outside your body.

**ELIZABETH STONE**

The time just before sleep is very important for children. How
they feel as they fall asleep can determine how they feel when
they wake up the next morning. Waking up in a good mood
can be a great shield for the entire day. Waking up in a foul
mood tends to attract negative experiences and emotions.
It's like the old saying: 'If you want to have a wonderful
tomorrow, then make the night before really special.'

For parents who have a tough time getting their children to
bed, telling them a story is a great solution. I believe one of
the primary reasons children do not look forward to bedtime
is that it holds no promise of activity. It is the end of activity, the
end of fun for the day, and activity and attention are what
they crave. Even if the adults are going to stay up longer,

engaging the children in a story provides closure for their day. During the pre-teen years, children crave activity with their parents. Creating great bedtime stories turns bedtime into a true parent–child activity. When it is done well, the child looks forward to bedtime, both for the story and for the ritual of formally closing the day with the happiest thoughts from that day.

It can be helpful to explain why adults get to stay up a bit later to do adult things. Children need to do their stuff and adults need to do theirs (paying bills, discussing things, planning and relaxing together). Let children know that, as they get older, you will show them these things when they are ready. In order for adults to be happy, they need quality adult time. All adults need this, as will your children some day, to keep a healthy mind and spirit. Children should know they need to respect adults' needs and rights just as they want respect for their playtime and TV time, etc. You can even explain, when this is age-appropriate, that sometimes couples become unhappy when they do not get a chance to give each other attention, and that on many days the only time left is at the end of that day. For the health of the family, adults need time alone together to nourish one another with high quality 'adult time'.

A bedtime story can bring the day's events into focus and help children to acknowledge the emotions around these events. Doing this in a fun way that gets the children involved with the process helps them to bond with their parents and be ready and willing to sleep. It's a fun activity they'll come to associate with going to bed, so they are ready to relax and drift off to sleep. With time and practice, a nightly story makes bedtime seem less like a punishment and more like a fun activity that winds down the day in a predictable, pleasant way.

# PREPARATION

# Preparation

It's better to be prepared for an opportunity and not have one than to have an opportunity and not be prepared.

**WHITNEY YOUNG**

Your first step, before you even bring up the idea of bedtime stories, is to get prepared.

You probably have the makings of great stories all around you. You could make up stories or characters based on your child's favourite activity. When he was young, my son was totally obsessed with trains, so I created Tooty the Train. My daughter had a pet hamster named Hampy, so we had stories about Hampy. Most children love inanimate objects that come to life. This is one of the reasons the *Toy Story* films are so popular. There's something intriguing about things coming to life. Whatever your child is interested in can be developed into a character or characters. Examples would be Terry the Tuba, Cammy the Camera, Kicks the Football,

Thrashy the Skateboard, Hoops the Basketball, and on and on. As you will see, the characters will grow and develop their own personalities, just as we all do.

So have a think about your child's favourite activities. I suggest writing these on paper or on computer. Paper is easier and faster for some people. Next to each activity, list objects that are associated with it. For example, my daughter is absorbed with dance. A quick list of objects would be tap shoes, pointe shoes, leotards, dance bags, hair nets, scrunchies, leg warmers and a ballet barre. After idea storming objects (without judging whether they will work or not), you can begin trying out some names for them.

Let's just look at the first one, tap shoes. Possible names are Tappy, Taps, Clack and Stomp. Or you could call them Terrie, Tasha, Terence or Tammy. Just have some fun when you do this. There is no right or wrong. They are just ideas. Nothing is carved in stone (yet). Make a list for each item. Try to get at least three for each, unless one is such a gem that you know it will be great.

Here's a list of mechanical devices that can lend themselves to characters: cars, planes, trains, bicycles, motorcycles, skateboards, wheelchairs, roller skates, roller blades, a bus, street car, tram, cable car, pogo stick, rocket, tractor, wagon, snowboard, boat, jet ski, snow skis, sled, toboggan, ice skates, helicopter, kite, hot-air balloon, hovercraft, tank, limo, SUV, people-carrier, fire engine, tricycle, truck, crane, monorail, biplane, triplane, blimp, taxi, rickshaw, dune buggy or an ATV (All-Terrain Vehicle).

Your characters can also have families and friends. You are creating a world of characters in the same way television programmes introduce a cast of interesting characters. Just like situation comedies, soap operas or dramas, your characters will have episodes involving adventure, comedy and strange situations. In the same way as you look forward to your favourite shows or books, your children will look forward to their bedtime story with anticipation and delight.

## Time for Bed

I suggest making a bedtime checklist. Include everything. That way there's no last-minute surprises to interrupt the process. Here are some ideas (in no particular order): teeth, shower or bath, hands, face, feet, a drink, prayers, hugs to others, homework, school things, stuff put away (games, toys, food, books, DVDs), pets fed or brushed. We sometimes put out clothes for the next day. This is great if you ever feel disorganized in the morning. If you normally spend time searching for those elusive socks, tights or knickers while the breakfast is burning, then organizing them at night is far less stressful. One advantage of putting out clothes the night before is that they have a better chance of matching. In the dim light of morning (and with a dim brain) I once wore dark blue trousers with a black jacket. I swear they were the same colour when I blearily took them from my wardrobe! Laying things out the night before would have been far more clever.

Now, back to your story preparation. Write out a few plot lines first. If you can't write it, you probably can't speak it. If you like talking, then pretend you are with your child and go for it. Then write down the key points as a framework. Do a few of these, and stretch yourself to see what you can come up with. Make sure you are having fun while you do this. The main point of all this is to have fun while bonding with and teaching your child. Wait for the opportune moment and announce that you want to tell your child a story.

## Feeling Anxious?

It's all right to have butterflies in your stomach.
Just get them to fly in formation.

**DR ROB GILBERT**

Perhaps you're feeling like you can't do this. You may be feeling inadequate for the job. That's normal. Reading from a book is simple. Anyone who can read can do that. While I will admit that telling your own story is more involved, and often puts you on the spot, it's not quite the same as public speaking (the number-one fear in Western societies for over 50 years, so they say). No matter what happens, your children will grow to love the stories you create together. Whether it starts off a smashing success or leaves you with a smashed ego, it will be great soon enough. Any time you spend with your children is good. Commit to doing it for one month before you judge its worth. After a month you will know for certain whether your children are getting into it. You'll loosen up after the first few stories. Or you may warm to it immediately! Either way, I'm sure you have overcome worse scenarios in your lifetime. Just start off doing it purely for entertainment. Later you can begin weaving in the various lessons about morals, science and whatever else you decide (we'll talk more about this in later chapters). For now, take a deep breath, put a smile on your face, and have a load of fun.

You will do foolish things, but do them
with enthusiasm.

**COLETTE**

Do the thing trembling if you must; but do it!

**EMMETT FOX**

Now let's talk about visualization.

# VISUALIZATION

# Visualization

Ordinary people believe only in the possible.
Extraordinary people visualize not what is possible
or probable, but rather what is impossible.
And by visualizing the impossible, they begin
to see it as possible.

**CHERIE CARTER-SCOTT**

Never underestimate the power of *seeing* what you are going to do before you do it. In fact, the best thing is to see your end result first. If you know where you are going, and you see yourself already there, the path tends to open up for you. This is what top athletes and businesspeople do. I heard an Olympic gold medal-winner say he saw himself standing on the podium receiving that heavy medal before the competition began. Now that's a great example of visualization! He got it spot-on. Earning the gold medal was the prime reason he was there. If he was not striving for gold, why was he bothering? I'm not saying silver and bronze medal-winners should not be proud and thrilled. However, what would you think of someone who qualified for the Olympics, made the journey halfway around the world, and then proclaimed they were really hoping for bronze? It just doesn't make sense. If that's all they can see, then the only way to earn gold is for everyone else to fall on their face. If you want to be the best, it certainly helps to see yourself as the best. If you want your children to be their best, then when they compete, even with themselves, gently teach them how to see themselves as successful.

In sports, athletes either see themselves in the winner's circle, as described above, or they see themselves performing extremely well. They will close their eyes and go through each movement, experiencing it in glorious perfection. They may do it in real time or slow it down to feel every muscle doing its part in harmony with the others. They actually see in their mind's eye their body as it manoeuvres itself as needed in their particular sport. If it's a physically competitive sport, they may choose to see themselves defeating their opponent. A fencer may see himself lunging and touching his opponent. A wrestler may see herself pinning her opponent to the mat. Each will review the moves in as high detail as they can. A rather famous account is of basketball players splitting into two groups. One group went onto the court and practised shooting baskets for 20 minutes. The other group sat and practised perfect free throws in their heads. When both groups went out to shoot, the visualizing group did just as well as the group who actually took the shots. With more practice getting better in their heads, they eventually outperformed the other group.

In business, people visualize their monetary success. Salesmen will see themselves living in the kind of house they want, or driving the kind of car they want. Tom Monahan, the owner of Domino's Pizza, reports that he built his empire using the power of visualization. Once I saw myself depositing a big cheque in the bank. A few months later a large corporate company issued me a huge cheque that gave me enough money for a down-payment on a house. Try this method and you will be surprised at how often your vision comes to be. It can work for material items as well as with less tangible things like relationships.

> I always wanted to be somebody, but I see now I should have been more specific.
>
> **LILY TOMLIN**

In medicine, people have been able to assist their healing by visualizing themselves well. One account tells us of people visualizing having millions more white blood cells to attack their infection. Blood analysis later showed a higher rate of infection-fighting cells than before their visualization. Somehow the concept was relayed from the brain to the body.

A friend's mother was diagnosed with cancer a few years back. He asked her to see thousands of little tanks blowing up the cancerous cells. She went into remission and felt better for a long time. Perhaps it was simply a psychological boost, but many times tests show impressive results. You can read about such things on the Internet. In any case, if you ever have a disease, it costs nothing to see these things and, as long as you are also following your doctor's advice, it can certainly do no harm to picture yourself feeling better. The medical community has long known that a person's attitude can affect their recovery. Those with a positive attitude tend to recover faster than those who are pessimistic about their future. Visualizing is a concrete way to express your optimism.

My suggestion is that you see yourself delivering your stories well. See them getting a warm reception from your children. See yourself smiling and happy because you transcended mere storytelling into story creating. Use this powerful visualization technique to get used to the idea before you do it. Some people feel that seeing yourself being able to perform certain tasks helps because we get used to the idea that we can actually do it! Once we are comfortable with it in our head, it's easier to manifest it in our lives.

> Losers visualize the penalties of failure;
> winners visualize the rewards of success.

**DR ROB GILBERT**

The next section is a bonus from my 'Goal Achievement' programme.

## How to Visualize

If I were there with you, I would ask you to close your eyes. I'd wait a few seconds and simply say, 'Big Ben'. Close your eyes and think about Big Ben right now for 10 seconds. Now open your eyes. What was happening in your mind? Did you see the tower with the clock? My guess is that when you closed your eyes your mind went immediately to a picture of Big Ben. In your mind, you probably did NOT see the letters: B – I – G  B – E – N. Am I correct? This is even more powerful when done in person. You even saw the letters printed in the book, yet probably did not see them in your mind's eye. That is because our brain works primarily with pictures.

In the same way, a well-told story creates vivid pictures in the mind of the listener. When you tell your stories, use words that convey what you see in your mind. Use powerful words to describe how big something is. Use words like huge, tremendous, colossal and gigantic. Your child will learn the meaning of these words through the way you use them. It will also create scale so your child understands exactly what is happening.

I'm going to reveal to you how to become great at visualizing. This is another wonderful activity you can do with your children. It's a fun game that will strengthen their ability to see with their mind. The result will be better problem-solving skills and more self-confidence and personal levels of achievement. The idea is very simple. Get very good at seeing pictures and you will become very good at keeping pictures in your mind. And when you can keep vivid pictures in your mind, your brain zeroes in on the solutions and paths to get you there. It's like giving the scent to a bloodhound. Visualization is like giving a 'pictorial scent' to your brain.

The way to become excellent at visualizing is to practise remembering pictures. Open a magazine to a random page without looking at it. With your eyes closed, bring the page up close to your face at a comfortable reading distance. Then do a 'visual snapshot': Open your eyes for half a second. Then close them. It's just a bit longer than a blink. With your eyes closed, or the page turned over, recall what you saw. If you can remember more than three or four main objects, then your eyes were open too long. If you remember a lot of detail, your eyes were definitely open too long! You should only have a vague concept of the page. For some people this is bothersome. They want to be perfect and not miss anything. That is not the point here. You want to miss almost everything. There may be 50 items on the page, but you only want the two or three main ones. Your response should sound like this: 'The top of the page was blue.

There was a picture on the bottom; I think it was at a beach. There was a headline in big white letters – something about a holiday. I think there was a palm tree on the right side.' If you know more than that, your eyes were open too long!

Now you repeat those steps, only this time look at the page for 5 seconds. Recall what you can, repeating the first few items, with any corrections. Then do that looking at the page for 10 seconds. Recall everything you can. Do it again for another 10-second look. Recall everything you can, adding as many fine details as you can. Repeat the process until you have almost every item on the page. You may do four or more 10-second sessions. Here are some helpful hints about the process:

1. Talk to yourself while looking at the page. Say what you are seeing – label things. Do a running commentary on what you see.
2. Do not read small print – only headlines or large captions. Just be able to say, 'There is a box of text in the lower left corner.'
3. Keep repeating the process until you can identify virtually everything on the page. Start with simple pages and work up to more complex ones.
4. You will be able to achieve a level of detail that will surprise you. You should know colours of clothing, logos, text and objects. You should know how many buttons are on a jacket or how many bowls of ice-cream are on a table. This is what I call getting to really fine levels of detail. After doing a few pictures, you will become quite adept.

It's fun to do this with another person and quiz each other afterward. The best way is for one person to go completely through the process, with the other person then quizzing them. Then switch roles. Do *not* do the visual snapshot, recall, then have your partner do their visual snapshot. That weakens the process. Take a complete turn with several repetitions, and then switch roles. A good method is to have your partner pick a page and hold it in front of you for the visual snapshot. After that, they can time your 5-second and 10-second sessions and take the magazine away from you each time. You do not need a stopwatch for this. Counting in your head or looking at your watch is fine. Do a couple of these exercises each day. Each session only takes a few minutes. I have found that doing this process also has the added benefit of reducing stress. Working with pictures in your mind activates the non-judgemental part of your brain. When we are removed from critical judgement we relax. As William Shakespeare said, 'There is nothing either good or bad, but thinking makes it so.'

The idea is to do this with your child. You can use fun pages from children's magazines or their school textbooks. Mix it up. It will make their schoolbook seem more fun, and they will actually absorb information along the way. You can also practise this technique while window-shopping, or in the car, or by stopping a movie on your TV (DVD works best). You can fast-forward and then stop in a random place. Then either turn away, close your eyes or use the TV remote to leave the DVD input. The exact method will depend on the number of remote controls you have! You can also use the Internet to search for images on browsers such as Google. Click the Images icon, type in a word, and search. Click on the image. At the top you will see 'Image has been scaled down. See full-size image.' Click there and it will enlarge the image for you. Visualizing pages is a great pastime while waiting in the doctor's surgery or at the airport. It's easy, you lose track of time, and it's fun.

You can make it a contest to see who can remember the most. Have a third person hold the page open for the sessions, and quiz you at the appropriate time. They can ask really difficult questions, and the first person to get 10 correct wins! As long as you can get someone to volunteer to ask the questions, you can have as many of you play as can easily see the page. You can add a twist to the game by interrupting the process at the end. Sit in a circle (or close to it) after the third or fourth 10-second session and take turns naming objects in your home. There can be no repeats. Do this for 1 or 2 minutes. Now go back to the remembering page. The time and interruption of seeing other pictures will degrade your memory of the page you were working on. This adds another level of difficulty to the game. It's fun to see how adults do against children. Children have the advantage of a less cluttered mind and a youthful brain. Adults may know more objects and be able to label them better. Adults may be able to focus for a longer time. Who will win? The answer is everyone, because it's fun, entertaining and serves a useful purpose.

Another positive aspect for adults is that research shows that one way to avoid mental deterioration is to keep the mind active. Crossword puzzles and games such as Boggle and Scrabble are often mentioned. Picture visualization stimulates both the visual and verbal parts of the brain in a synergistic way. It's also easier to do than a crossword or round of Scrabble if you are a bit tired. It's faster paced and anyone can do it almost anywhere they go. You can also teach it to others very quickly.

# CREATING AND DEVELOPING CHARACTERS

# Creating and Developing Characters

Your stories will benefit from a cadre of characters who appear in most of your stories. With our family, each child had a main character who was in virtually every story. Hampy the Hamster usually came in near the very end, surprising everyone by being behind the plot from the beginning. The first time this happened there was huge fleet of thousands of starships spanning a huge section of outer space. Bristling with powerful weapons, they formed a gigantic sphere. In the middle was the mother ship, twice the size of the earth. Our heroes were led through a maze of golden tunnels, past huge doors, county-sized sports arenas and glistening cities. Finally they came to the palace, which was made of diamonds and every precious gem and mineral you could name. There were statues thousands of meters tall, and large chamber after chamber, until finally they reached the inner sanctum, which itself was the size of a large convention centre. There were golden steps leading up to a magnificent throne carved from platinum in the shape of a starburst. It had finely detailed frescoes and statues embedded into it. The scene was overpoweringly magnificent. On the seat of the throne was a huge cushion made from the silk of a rare creature from a distant planet, so soft and cushiony that beings sold entire planets just to have a small sample on order. After climbing the 1,001 steps, our heroes finally arrived to meet the ruler of this magnificent and powerful civilization. At first there seemed to be nobody there. Then they heard a faint scratching sound, and up onto the cushion jumped a familiar sight. It was their little friend Hampy! Tooty was almost speechless. 'Hampy! W-W-What are you doing here?'

'Oh, hi guys! What am I doing here? I'm the ruler and all-powerful eternal Queen here. Why?'

The conversation continued, with the visitors learning that Hampy had not only designed everything, but had built the fleet in her spare time when she wasn't running on her little wheel in her cage back on Earth. Hampy had even designed the throne, though she had someone else build it. When asked how she could possibly have had time to do all these things, she responded by saying that a person has to keep busy! Anyway, after the shock had worn off, the others pleaded their case to her, and she instantly granted their wish. Hampy was always generous and would do anything to help others.

This story helped define the character of Hampy's personality and her penchant for ending up in the maddest situations. Eventually in our storytelling sessions, whenever there was something amazing about to happen the children usually guessed ahead of time that Hampy would be involved. Every once in a while I would switch things around to keep them on their toes. I would mention little clues that made it *seem* like it would be Hampy, but these would turn out to be false leads. Many of the stories turned into what some might call mysteries or detective stories. There were clues and telltale signs that pointed in a certain direction. Sometimes these would be reliable, but other times purposely misleading. However, I always made sure that there was a method to the madness. Once there was some bedding material present where someone was last seen. That would point to Hampy being involved (hamsters like shredding up material to make a cosy bed for themselves). But sometimes it turned out that Hampy was also trying to find out what was going on, and was not the culprit herself. The times that most challenged me were when the children guessed my plot and I had to change the ending during the telling. Coming up with alternative plots without breaking stride was exhilarating. I loved it. Most of the time I was able to pull it off and redeem the situation. A few times they said my endings were 'lame', but that also made them feel good because they had thought of something that even the 'great Dad' could not fully recover from. I tried to show them that it was better to try and fail than to not give it any effort at all.

> 100% of shots not taken never score.
>
> **WAYNE GRETSKY (RENOWNED ICE HOCKEY PLAYER)**

When developing your characters, I suggest sometimes giving them personalities and physical traits that go counter to what would be expected. If they are a creature that is usually shy, make them really bold instead. That gives you the opening to discuss how they would have trouble fitting in with their own kind. They might be seen as 'different' and be somewhat shunned in their society. If you want to cover a theme about independence, or about conformity, that's a great place to start.

Remember, I see these stories as a way to instil your values and beliefs in your children. I would like to take a moment to address those people who feel that it's wrong to do that.

We all develop beliefs, values and attitudes. We get them from television, films, books and, most of all, from other people. Do you really trust others to handle this for you? I'm not saying to pound your children over the head with it. That usually doesn't work. Eventually they will rebel. Just be true to your heart; and make it fun. They'll get the idea.

Another way I developed characters was to give them ambitions and goals that were seriously beyond their natural capabilities. Imagine a worm whose dream was to fly. Or picture a whale who wanted to do ballet. How about a robot who wanted to be in love? What about a bull who wanted to work in a china shop? Oh – that reminds me – you can invent plots by using old sayings. I think it's really cool when little children understand old sayings. This is a great way to teach them things you know from bygone times. I have observed that adults are very impressed with children who know about things that are from a time before they were born. As a dancer, my daughter is familiar with music from every decade. We were at someone's home and they were playing swing music. She not only knew the song but how to dance to it. Our hosts were quite impressed and I felt very proud. I think that people who only know about one small slice of culture are limited in their thinking and become boring quickly. I would say the same thing for any subject. It's good to know about diverse subjects for many reasons. Bedtime stories provide a great format for exposing your children to ideas and information they can't really get any other way.

Most writers will tell you to write about what you know best, or know well. That advice is good for telling bedtime stories too. Your characters will usually reflect some aspects of yourself. They are your alter egos. You can vicariously live adventures through them and take your children along for the ride. Since your children will help you to develop them, they will be a combination of both your personalities. With characters like that, how can you possibly go wrong?

The main character can go to bed at the end, safe and sound. They end up just like your child, all snuggled into bed (except when you want to end with a cliffhanger!).

The story can revolve around what happened that day (events, sports, lessons, TV programmes, school), but does not always have to, or that can be a starting point. Or the plot can end up addressing one of these events or situations at the end. The story can be about anticipating something coming up (film, holiday, guest, project, etc.).

## Characters Staying True over Time

Give your characters traits and reactions the children can depend on over time. If they act out of character, make it for a good reason. Characters can develop new skills and abilities, but their basic nature should remain constant over time. A good model would be the *Sesame Street* character, Elmo. Elmo is always happy and positive no matter what. There has never been an episode where Elmo is vindictive or mean-spirited. He is always true to himself. Your characters should generally be that way too. I'm not saying they cannot get sad or be angry. We'll cover that later. I'm saying that it's better when your characters are consistent.

Now, you can *sometimes* fool your child with a clever deception. Let's say that Tappy is usually very happy and talkative. We could have a situation where for some reason Tappy is acting out of character. The reason could be that Tappy is sad, or it could turn out to be Tappy's long-lost twin. As you will see, when you use your imagination, anything is possible. If you or your children like science fiction or fantasy, you can borrow ideas from films, books and TV programmes you have seen.

If you change a character, make sure it's for a good reason. Otherwise, your stories will not be consistent over time. Your child will remember a lot of detail, especially once they are older and more sophisticated. Of course, your stories will vary in sophistication depending on the mental and emotional development of your child. You would probably not be using the concept of alternate dimensions with a four-year-old. With a ten-year-old it's a different story.

Another aspect to keep straight is the *relationships* between characters. As with any story, characters who are friends should not be strangers the next time. Any knowledge or skills they have gained should be intact the next time they join the story. Treat them like real people (with wild super powers) and you'll be fine. I know this is probably common sense, but I would be remiss if I didn't mention it.

My belief is that most children would be upset if characters were inconsistent without purpose. I'm told that children like a high degree of consistency and predictability in their world. Psychologists mostly agree that children in environments where they cannot predict how their parent(s) will act or react develop trust issues all through their lives. Unstable environments can lead to unstable personalities.

Children of inconsistent parents tend to exhibit more fear and have less confidence than children who have experienced more stable parents.

## Introducing New Characters

The only real voyage of discovery consists not in seeking new landscapes but in having new eyes.

**MARCEL PROUST**

Introducing new characters into your stories will depend a lot on your child. Some children will just want you to handle the whole thing. Others will want a lot of control or input. Some may want you to provide the *type* of character (fish, drum, airplane) and then they will want to come up with the name. The same child may want it one way today and differently tomorrow. The key is to be flexible and go with the flow. Remember, this is their story. Sometimes you will really want to go a certain way, and they will want something else. You may have to negotiate with them. There were times when I really wanted to go on about a specific idea and they protested. Sometimes I would relent and go with their thoughts. Other times I explained that I had a particular idea to share with them, and that if they did not like it, tomorrow night I would do their version.

The point is not to get too attached to your characters or ideas. This is a time for quiet fun and bonding, not for being a control freak. The odds are that most of the time you will be tired after a long day. This is meant to be a *break* from that. You are spending quality time with your child. You are letting go and having some fun. You are also transitioning from your shared world to your adult world.

This is the last child-dominated activity of the day. After this, whatever time is left is for you and your significant other. If you are a single parent with no other adult around, this is the break you've earned today. You have paid your daily dues and been a loving caregiver. After the story it's time to kick back.

Once you've told a number of these stories, introducing new characters is easy. Your main character (or anyone else) can bump into them or discover them in any of a dozen ways. They can see them coming from a distance, hear them making some strange sounds, be introduced by another character (this is a good opportunity to teach your child how to make introductions) or simply find them in some strange place. If one character is introducing another, they can either do it very well or they can get all tongue-tied and not know what to do. Later another character can explain to the first one how to introduce others properly. Your child will learn through example, without having the stress of doing it for real. Or worse, they can be humiliated by being told they messed it up in public. Now that's a great way to start off a friendship: being corrected by your parents in front of your new friend.

## The First Time

The first time you tell a bedtime story, you need a different strategy, since there are no characters at all yet. The process can sound something like this:

'OK, let's have a bedtime story. I've got an idea about a tap shoe named Tappy. Would you like to hear it?'

'OK!'

Now is when you lay down the expectation that, once they have gone and washed up, cleaned their teeth, got into their pyjamas, etc., you will tell them the story of Tappy the Tap Shoe. Ten minutes later …

'Once upon a time, there was a funny little tap shoe. His/her name was Tappy. Tappy loved to dance, just like you. Tappy was always happiest when s/he was hitting the floor, making that wonderful clacking sound. S/he had good metal taps, which were not too loose and not too tight. Whenever s/he sat in the dance bag, s/he would dream about dancing again. While some shoes would be lonely waiting, Tappy was never sad. S/he always figured out new ways to get better and better. Tappy would always stretch to stay supple so s/he would fit just right – not too loose and not too tight.'

From that point Tappy could begin an adventure (accidentally picked up by another dancer, put on the wrong foot, misplaced, has a song stuck in his/her head, etc.). Tappy could have a twin or a friend s/he always dances with. They could be Tappy and Happy, or Tappy and Scrappy, or whatever you like. This is a time when you can choose a name for the next character together (co-operative storytelling). Often a name can reflect a personality trait, as with the Seven Dwarfs (Grumpy is grumpy, Sleepy is always tired, etc.). Scrappy could have a very independent nature, always wanting to dance to a different beat or song. This could be used to explain why sometimes the dancer seems to be making mistakes!

## Giving Characters Different Voices

One of the strongest characteristics of genius
is the power of lighting its own fire.

**JOHN W. FOSTER**

When you create a character, you can give it a special voice. It can be soft, gravelly, high-pitched, mystical-sounding or slow. It can have an accent or a lisp, be overly excited or mechanical. This will add an extra dimension to the story and will usually make children laugh. And for Pete's sake, do not be embarrassed. These are your children! Have fun with them while you can. Soon they will be in college and married. Before that they will be teenagers. This is the time to snuggle up and show them they are totally loved and that there's nothing you would not do for them. Show them that you will even do silly voices – especially if you are not very good at it! If it's that bad, they'll ask you to stop. I can speak from personal experience ...

At first I practised voices ahead of time. After a while I let the children decide how they wanted the voice. They would tell me to make my voice lower or higher, or faster or slower. Sometimes I could not do it if I had been lecturing all day. Sometimes I got the voices mixed up and they'd tell me I'd got it wrong. That was when I realized they were actually paying attention! A couple of times I had a mild cold and could not hit the high-pitched ones. Either they would do it for me or they'd settle for the best I could do. Once I had a very sore throat and I whispered the important lines and my daughter said them aloud for me. It was a good lesson for her in listening. It made it a bit difficult for me to keep track of where I was in the story – it felt like when a mobile phone bounces your voice back to you about a second later – and because it was so disconcerting my daughter had to keep reminding me of where we were in the story. The fact that I could hardly keep my eyes open probably didn't help much, either!

Back in the 1980s and '90s, the impressionist Rich Little (he is almost as talented as Rory Bremner) claimed that he was far more clever and funny when impersonating Johnny Carson (the then comedic host of *The Tonight Show*). Somehow imitating that great comedian put him in touch with something in himself that brought him to a higher level. Personally, I've found that a story is much easier to tell and flows better when I do different voices. I feel more like the characters and say things I'm not sure I would think of as just myself. I've heard actors say the same thing about when they really get into character. They ad lib in a way that is more consistent with their character than they would be themselves. I believe that you will feel the same once you get into it.

> Setting a good example for your children does nothing but increase their embarrassment.
>
> **DOUG LARSON**

## Cameo Appearances

A fun thing to do is to introduce other characters your child knows into your stories. These characters can either play a small role or they can be a major part of the plot. They can come from cartoons, sitcoms, movies, books or wherever. They can even be one of their friends or a teacher at school. Anyone is fair game, as long as you respect the person in the story. I do not advocate ridiculing a person in a story, as that teaches children the wrong lesson about how to interact with people. Usually we would bring in a particular person or character when their personality fitted the situation. If your child has a 'weird' friend, then sometimes it can very funny to put that person in a situation where they bumble into a solution that saves the day. We may be poking fun a bit, but we are not mocking them. If it is done in a loving and respectful way, then I think it's OK. I will admit that sometimes my children and I pushed the limits of what's appropriate. My guideline was that I did not say anything I would not have said if the person were there in the room.

A cameo appearance can be very effective near the end of a story. Once there was a beautiful planet with many gardens and palaces. When we finally met the ruler of this planet it turned out to be one of my daughter's close friends. It was a great surprise and quite silly. We laughed about it for a week and told her friend a couple of days later when we went out for ice-cream. She was delighted to know she was of royal heritage and had hundreds of loyal servants. Although it was fantasy, I believe she was very pleased that we thought of her that way. I think she also felt honoured to be included in one of our famous bedtime stories.

Once word got round, other friends wanted to be included in a story. This was really great, because it gave me ideas for several weeks. Some of them even gave me ideas to use. It turned into a friendly game of who got made into the coolest character.

Your stories can also involve relatives. It might be nice to have Grandpa or Aunt Jane appear in one of the adventures. It's probably a great idea to have them shown in a positive light. Experience suggests that children repeat things. Whatever Uncle Phil does in the story will probably get back to Phil rather quickly. This is especially true if it was less than flattering. Bad news travels fast! If you've had a row with someone, either leave them out of it or use it as a way of letting your child know that you don't hold grudges. Let's not teach our children to hold grudges. It's not healthy, either physically or emotionally.

Resentment is like taking poison and waiting for the other person to die.

**MALACHI McCOURT**

# CREATIVITY

# Creativity

If you can't excel with talent, triumph with effort.

**DAVE WEINBAUM**

One big advantage of learning to be more creative is that it will help you in your professional life. Whenever the brain gets exercise, the effect spills over into everything you do. You will find new ideas popping up all the time. Ideas will come to you while you are driving, showering, walking, talking, eating, or possibly even during a meeting. The more we exercise, the stronger we get. This is true both physically and mentally. The more you practise creativity, the more creative you become.

Since children tend to model their parents, demonstrating the willingness to be creative sends a message to your child that it's OK and good to be creative. Being creative means taking a risk. Many people deny or suppress their creativity because when they were young somebody mocked their efforts. It became safer to do nothing. Consider a new twist on an old saying: 'Nothing ventured, nothing pained.' Any fool can work hard. Working smarter usually means being creative in some way. People who find solutions to plaguing problems are paid big money and get a lot of respect. I believe that people who suppress their creativity tend to live lives that can be easily copied by anyone. If you want to make a difference in the world, it takes some degree of creativity. You need to look at things a bit differently from others.

You can start small. Once you get momentum going, you'll be surprised at how you begin to see new relationships between seemingly unrelated things. While this skill is not a prerequisite for success, you are stronger with it than without it. And the best way to foster creativity is to let go and not be concerned with anyone else's opinion.

> Man is most nearly himself when he achieves the seriousness of a child at play.
>
> **HEROCLITUS**

Do not worry about creativity. You may be thinking, 'I'm just not creative.' Maybe you are and maybe you're not. It really doesn't matter (much). Your child probably is, and it's likely there's a creative part of you that's been hidden for a while. Like a dormant seed, it only needs light and a little nurturing. With the help of your child, you will create a wonderful world of loveable characters that will always have a special meaning for you both.

Make sure your child is actively involved in the process of creating both the characters and the stories. There may come a time when you ask what tonight's story should be about and they want to leave it up to you. By that time you'll be an old hand at this and you'll start suggesting possibilities. They may veto one or two, but you'll hit the mark pretty quickly. Even when you are tired, your brain will surprise you with many possibilities. After a few attempts, your child will jump in and save you.

Before you begin a story, it's a good idea to take a few moments and visualize yourself finishing up and both of you (or all of you) being happy with the story. See smiles, hugs and a thank you from your 'audience'. When being creative, learn to just let go and see what happens. You will never be 'perfect' at this. If it ever feels like you are, it probably means you were not daring enough! Messing up is part of the process. There will be good times and less than good times. Unless you are a professional storyteller, your children will not expect works of genius every night; and neither should you. Just show up and do what you can.

> Creativity is allowing yourself to make mistakes.
> Art is knowing which one to keep.
>
> **SCOTT ADAMS**

Once you get going, ideas will start coming at odd times, as I said. May I suggest keeping a small notebook or voice recorder? Your mobile phone probably has a recording function (ask your children to show you ...). Ideas have a funny way of evaporating. In my goal course, our catchphrase is, 'Don't just think it – ink it!' Writing your ideas down will help. Recording them serves the same purpose. Make sure that later you commit your ideas to paper.

Even the palest ink is better than the best memory.

**CHINESE PROVERB**

There are also ways to be creative in the actual telling of your story. As Marshall McLuhan said back in the 1960s, 'The medium is the message.' You can vary certain elements of your delivery, such as the tone and pitch of your voice, your pacing (how slow or fast you speak), how animated you are (using hand gestures or walking like Frankenstein's monster, or pretending you're flying), and using sound effects (booms and gasps, the sound of ray guns and screams).

You can make use of props if you like, although you may want the story to only take place in your child's imagination. However, there may be times when you want to teach your children something that must be explained with a visual aid. For example, if you wanted them to know about how an eclipse takes place, you could use an apple for the Earth and a walnut for the moon and show them going around one another in front of a lamp. Then you could begin your story about how a gigantic swarm of crazed fruit flies made everyone think there was a lunar eclipse. I hardly ever made use of props myself, but it is a possibility. It depends on your personality and whether you want to put on more of a show. As long as the prop doesn't end up being a distraction, it's probably fine. If your child takes the prop and starts playing with it or hitting their brother or sister with it, the idea was probably best left on the drawing board. It's one of those calls you have to make yourself. Unless you really develop using props into an art, it's probably best used sparingly. The imagination is far more powerful than a real object.

# KEEPING IT CO-OPERATIVE: GETTING THE CHILDREN INVOLVED

# Keeping It Co-operative: Getting the Children Involved

Let early education be a sort of amusement.
You will then be better able to find out the natural
bent of the child.

**PLATO**

The goal here is to co-create the story with your child. Some children like more participation than others, and this can also vary from night to night. You will need to play it one day at a time to see whether, and how, they want to join in. Some nights they will be brimming with ideas and really excited; other times they will be tired and want you to handle the whole thing. Either way, the process works. The point is that you are together and having fun, which leads to a co-operative 'getting tucked in'. The beauty of the process is that it ends with a hug and a kiss and there's no more that needs to happen, other than 'I love you.'

## Inappropriate Requests

If your child starts asking for the characters to do things you do not approve of, I would suggest discussing it. Let's say a child asks for a character to do something overtly violent. Your first impulse may be to criticize, but this will most likely result in rebellion and destructive feelings. Before you get to that point, you have an opportunity to learn something important and insightful about the child. In the next few minutes you may be able to avoid spending thousands on future counselling sessions! So, you can either make a non-threatening observation, or ask (in a neutral tone) why they want the violent act to happen. The answer will be revealing. Perhaps it's as simple as something they saw on TV, or something they heard a classmate talking about. In that case, you can intercede and explain why you feel that would be inappropriate. If they are harbouring some deep-seated anger, you can gently pursue a dialogue that will let you know what's going on with them. It may not be easy, but the idea is to remain calm and not emotionalize the situation. Emotion-alizing actions seals them into memory. Here's an example:

Parent: 'What should Squishy do next?'

Child: *'He should chop the guy's head off and eat it!'*

Parent: 'Hmmm, Squishy has never done anything like that before ...'

Child: *'I know. But I want him to do it now.'*

Parent: 'How would that help the situation?'

Child: *'Then the guy wouldn't bother them at their picnic.'*

Parent: 'You make a good point. The guy would not bother them.'

**Child:** *'Yeah!'*

**Parent:** 'Squishy always gets along so well with everyone. I wonder, would Squishy have as much fun with a dead guy lying there?'

At this point, the child can go either way. They could relent and realize it was not such a good idea. Or they could be stubborn and hold their ground. If this happens, and they really mean it, you may not be able to avoid the counsellor. But let's proceed with the less violent conclusion.

**Child:** *'No, I didn't think about that. It would be pretty gross.'*

**Parent:** 'How else could they have fun at the picnic, and still have the guy there?'

**Child:** *'They could ask him to join them. Then they could all have some fun.'*

**Parent:** 'I like your idea. It's very friendly and shows good manners. Perhaps the guy could bring some food they never had before.'

**Child:** *'Yeah. That sounds good. Maybe he has some ice-cream that never melts until you eat it!'*

**Parent:** 'What a great idea! I like the way you think. Maybe this weekend we should get some ice-cream!'

**Child:** *'That sounds really good. Can we get back to the story now?'*

**Parent:** 'OK. So Squishy asked if the newcomer would like to join them ...'

In this scenario the parent did not find out where the child got the scary idea. The parent could simply have asked, 'That's quite a dramatic idea. Where did you hear about something like that?' It was probably either another child or a TV special about head-hunters. Either way, you can let your feelings come through in a non-threatening or non-critical way. (Note, the parent does not say, 'Where did you get such a *horrible* idea?') If you do not address it at all, you give it your approval by default. If the child makes a big deal about it, you could explain why such ideas are destructive and inappropriate, especially before bedtime. I suggest that this be said in a kind way, and not in a degrading or judgemental manner. I learned a long time ago that anything you emotionalize you tend to get more of. That's true for things you emotionalize in yourself and in others. I'd suggest calmly trying to uncover the roots of such an idea without arousing suspicion or a big reaction.

Of course, you are free to say anything you want. This is your child, after all. You could say something like, 'Oh! That's really disgusting! How could you even think of such a terrible thing?' But know that this is a great way to shut down creativity and diminish self-worth. The idea was creative, although in poor taste. I think part of being a parent is guiding our children towards socially acceptable thinking without squashing their creativity. Creativity is a tool, like a hammer. With a hammer you can build a school or you can hit someone on the head. By itself the hammer is just a tool full of great potential. It's up to us to make builders and not bullies.

## Involving Children in the Decisions

If you want to build a ship, don't drum up people together to collect wood and don't assign them tasks and work, but rather teach them to long for the endless immensity of the sea.

**ANTOINE DE SAINT-EXUPÉRY**

In some ways these are your stories, and in some ways they belong to both of you (or all of you if you're creating stories for several children at once). While there will be times when your children are too tired to participate, most of the time they will delight in coming up with ideas and characters together with you. Even when they are tired, you can still ask them questions to keep them involved. For example, let's say you create a character who is a worm. You could ask your children if they want it to have a high-pitched or low-pitched voice. They could help decide whether the worm has an accent, and from where. You could ask them if they would like it to be long or short, and what colour. You can ask them if they would like it have a certain special power, or be an ordinary worm. Perhaps it only does mime.

The reason for involving your children is threefold. One is to promote creativity. The first step in being creative is the *willingness* to be creative. Even if you believe you are not a creative person, you can still put in the effort. If you truly feel you cannot model creativity, simply model *attempting* to be creative. My guess is that you will eventually surprise yourself. Be courageous and show your child that you are willing to put it on the line and possibly appear foolish. The only thing I can think of more foolish in this circumstance is giving up on yourself and displaying blatant fear in front of your child. Decide to have fun no matter what. Consider what education expert Karen Crocket has to say about this: 'Your worst humiliation is only someone else's momentary entertainment.'

The second reason is to bond. The characters and plots will be a combination of your imaginations. You will always share that with your children.

The third reason is to get them used to making decisions. Making good decisions is a keystone of life. If you want your child to be a leader, or an intelligent follower, they will need to feel at home making decisions. Giving them practice and praising their efforts are great ways to promote feeling good about taking on the responsibility of making decisions.

The next day (or even during the story) you can discuss any decisions that turned out to be problematic. Making decisions on the fly like this will lead to developments that sometimes make the story line hard to resolve. There will be unforeseen paradoxes and problems that will be caused by some of your mutual decisions (not to mention your own individual decisions!). Backtracking and figuring out together how to solve them will be fun, and help your child develop a sense of logic, creativity and critical thinking skills. Discussing why it was a poor decision gives you all the chance to learn from it outside regular life. Many of the poor decisions we make in life are not reversible. Getting practice with make-believe characters and situations is a safe way to explore the possibilities.

No matter how far you have gone on the
wrong road, turn back.

**AUTHOR UNKNOWN**

Some people say that one of the marks of a mature adult is the ability to recognize our mistakes and own them. Until we do this, we tend to not learn from our mistakes. If we do not learn from them, we will probably continue to make them over and over. Some people make mistakes because they don't take time to think. Other people make mistakes because they are not clear thinkers. Yet others make mistakes because they think about things too much, and either get confused or believe they must keep thinking until they have considered every possibility. These people are sometimes known as perfectionists. A long time ago I learned that there are only two kinds of perfectionists: 'former' and 'frustrated'. Perfection is a myth – a dangerous, horrible, debilitating myth.

> A good plan executed right now is better than
> a perfect plan executed next week.
>
> **GEORGE S. PATTON**

A key factor in becoming a successful adult is to be clear-thinking. If we can get into the habit of sound, reasoned thinking, our brain is more likely to provide us with good information during a crisis. If we are habitually lazy thinkers, we will probably just panic during an emergency. Confidence in our ability to see a situation clearly and think of solutions will pay off the more we need it to. Leaders are generally people who can think clearly and then get others to see their vision.

> Readers are plentiful; thinkers are rare.
>
> **HARRIET MARTINEAU**

There may come a time when your children want to tell a story themselves. This is very good. You may even want to institute a time when they do this. For instance, you could tell stories for nine nights and they could tell one on the tenth night. Another way to do it is to have them tell the story on a particular night of the week. Or it could be random, when the mood strikes them. If they know that Saturday night is *their* night to tell the story, then it teaches them to get prepared for it with ideas. However their story unfolds, praise should be heaped upon them. Think of it as bedtime karaoke.

# TRUSTING YOURSELF TO COME UP WITH IDEAS

# Trusting Yourself to Come Up with Ideas

Make your judgement trustworthy by trusting it.

**GLENVILLE KLEISER**

With my bedtime storytelling, many times I just started with no idea whatsoever of what I was going to say. I just went with it. It was sort of scary at first. Eventually I realized that either I would come up with something great or I wouldn't. It didn't really matter. The children knew that I was there for them. Sometimes they told me that a story was really not up to par. I would admit it and tell them it was the best I could do that night. They could replay one of their favourites in their mind if they wanted to. There's nothing like watching your favourite movie over and over!

On the other hand, some of the very best stories I ever told seemed to come out of thin air. I would just keep talking until an adventure came to life by itself. A few times it involved a totally new character. Several times I just came up with a plot that was quite inspired (if I do say so myself...). A few of them truly made me feel proud. On some of those, I got especially good reviews from the children. I would usually tell a story to my youngest, then go to my oldest (we had two) since he could stay up a bit longer. Sometimes I would tell the same one and sometimes not. I would get really excited when I told a great one, wanting to share it. Sometimes I would even tell my wife afterwards. Ah, those were the days!

The point is, *don't panic*. Just relax into it and trust. They may not all be gems, but they are superior to just reading from a book (which is fine, too). Reading to your children is an excellent thing to do, and it should be done every day as they are growing up. As a reading coach I would never suggest anything different. In fact, reading books a bit earlier gives you great material to use later in your bedtime stories!

> Man's mind, once stretched by a new idea,
> never regains its original dimensions.
>
> **OLIVER WENDELL HOLMES, JR**

There are hundreds of ideas all around you (probably thousands). Some are just fun, some are educational, others are cultural. An obvious source of ideas comes from what has happened that day in your child's life. For example, if there was a science fair at school, then one of your characters could visit the fair. They could have visited there unseen by everyone else or, if the exhibits are still up, they could be there as you tell the story. Or they could have their own science fair with wacky projects that do outrageous things. Another great source of ideas is the news. What is happening locally, nationally or internationally? This source provides a terrific way to make sure your children understand what is going on in the world. Again, be sure to use pleasant topics whenever possible. You can use your stories to deal with tragedies, but I would suggest being very careful not to contaminate the fun aspect of your bedtime stories. If something bad happens and your child does not want the bedtime story to deal with it, your characters can be far off on an adventure and know nothing about it. Sometimes burying our head in the sand is the best approach for young ones, especially just before sleep.

> Resolve to do each job in a relaxed way,
> with all your attention.
>
> **THICH NHAT HANH**

Once, one of my children was having a difficult time with maths. Our little hamster just happened to be struggling with a similar challenge! Can you imagine that? For some outrageous reason, she had to figure out the volume of her bedding material. The problem was compounded because, whenever she went back to make the next measurement, she kept fluffing it more, thereby changing the volume each time. She finally got another piece of bedding material and, when she felt the urge to fluff, she used the old one. She was so tired out after doing this for so many hours, it was a good thing she had fluffed up the original piece so thoroughly. 'It made a great bed and she soon fell fast asleep, just like you're going to do right now. So let's fluff up your pillow and I'll turn down my "volume" so you can fall to sleep.' ('Volume' got a well-deserved groan.)

You can also get ideas from books you are reading or articles you get online or at work. In fact, your career can be a source of inspiration as well. If you want your children to better understand what you do for a living, you can tell them about neutral things that happen there, or specific projects you are working on. You can mention them during the day, and that night or the next night you can include them in your story. Then the next day you can discuss other aspects of your work. Just be careful not to mention anything about people or any complaints you have about work. Children tend to repeat these things, and if they do repeat what they hear, you can be sure they will say it to the worst possible person at the worst possible time! I recall the time their mum took the children to 'Young Minds at Work Day'. She introduced our young son to her supervisor. The first words out of his mouth were, 'My mum says she works in a Dilbert cartoon.' How do you recover from *that* one? (If you are not familiar with the comic strip Dilbert, it deals with stereotypical workplace personalities and the lunacy which can occur in office settings.)

You can get ideas from fairy tales as well. Read to your children from such books and then borrow ideas, characters or plots for your stories. Another place to get ideas from is biographies (and, of course, autobiographies). It's a way to learn about important and influential people. You can incorporate your characters into the life of the person you read about, and those people can show up in your stories as well.

Yet another source for ideas is sport. There are always sporting events happening in every season. Since they have action, they lend themselves very well to storytelling. There is always human drama involved in sport as well. There are people who overcome disabilities and great odds to compete and carry the day. It's very easy to adapt these sometimes heroic efforts to your stories. Even if you are not a sport enthusiast, the lessons that can be learned are applicable to most other kinds of human effort.

There are also the funny foibles associated with sport. There are fumbles, slips, misses and a variety of slapstick misadventures that would be fun to include in your stories. Either the person who committed the mistake can visit your story or one of your characters can have the same thing happen to them. Or your character can visit the stadium, field, pitch or whatever. Either way it ties the two together. We can always learn lessons from other people.

> Some of us learn by other people's mistakes
> – the rest of us have to be the other people.
>
> **AUTHOR UNKNOWN**

One consideration in choosing a topic is to ask yourself why you are choosing that topic. Are your intentions to educate or entertain? Are they to encourage empathy? Are they to bond? The type of reason will determine where to get your inspiration, or what to do with it once you have it. Sometimes it's simply time for bed and the children want a story, in which case the closest category would be bonding. As Groucho Marx said, 'Sometimes a cigar is just a cigar.'

# LOCATION, LOCATION, LOCATION

# Location, Location, Location

May your trails be crooked, winding, lonesome,
dangerous, leading to the most amazing view.
May your mountains rise into and above the clouds.

**EDWARD ABBEY**

You may be thinking that this storytelling lark is a great way to have adventures. You're correct! However, every so often I like to throw a riddle into the mix, especially if there isn't time for a full-blown adventure. I might start off the story and then have the main character suddenly wonder where he is. The world would look very strange to him, and he wouldn't be able to figure out his location.

To give you an example:

Tooty was huffing and puffing along, but there was no sky. He looked up and could only see these huge hexagonal shapes stretching off into the distance. He was in a deep valley that rose up sharply on both sides. He travelled for quite a while and then came to a dead end. Where was he? He turned around and went the other way. Finally he reached the far end of the valley. It was the same thing. He was trapped! So he got out his Magic Dust and started flying up and up. When he rose above the valley, he saw huge brown and grey plateaux stretching out for what seemed like hundreds of miles. There seemed to be more valleys between them, some smaller and some bigger. Suddenly a huge monster was flying past him. Its wingspread must have been 50 feet! It looked like a gigantic mosquito. Wait a minute – it *was* a gigantic mosquito! Oh, Tooty must have accidentally spilled his shrinking powder. Can you guess where he was?

The answer was that Tooty was under the bed. The plateaux were the wooden floorboards, the cracks between the boards were the valleys. The large hexagonal shapes were the underside of the mattress. This was a great lesson in perspective, as well as a fun story. It only took a couple of minutes, but was satisfying enough. Once Tooty knew where he was, he was able to grow bigger and find the way to his bed in the roundhouse. 'And he snuggled under his blankets, just like you, and his daddy came and gave him a good night kiss, just like this. Good night.'

So we see that, while you can have exotic planets, islands and universes, sometimes you can just look round and find a new world right under your nose.

There's no place like home.

**L. FRANK BAUM,** The Wizard of Oz

You can also describe places you have been to on holiday, or your workplace, friends' houses, the car, the fridge, your child's hair, the garden, a computer keyboard, fingerprints, the tumble dryer, your shoes and on and on. Just look around and imagine what the world would look like if you were really, really tiny. If you've ever seen the film *Honey, I Shrunk the Kids* you'll know what I mean.

# SPECIAL POWERS, MAGIC AND TIME TRAVEL

# Special Powers, Magic and Time Travel

It's a lot of fun to assign special powers to at least some of your characters. It fuels your creativity. As long as you're having an adventure, you might as well take it to the max! Special powers can either be a natural part of the character or they can be something that artificially gives them power, like a suit that makes them invisible. Hampy the Hamster had a magic cape that allowed her to fly. This way she could usually be the first one to arrive in an emergency. The problem was that she did not have very good control over it. She would usually fly right past, calling out, 'Superhero Hampy, out to save the day ... Don't worry, everyone, I'm on my waaaaaay!' The last part faded out as she sped past the scene and out of sight. She did that every time she wore the magic cape. The children expected it, knew it was coming, and loved it, every time. It's just like when you know a certain line is coming in a film: you're sure it's coming, but it's done well and it works. This was the same. I did Hampy's voice as high and squeaky as I could manage, and in my mind I'd see a group of people waiting to be saved, like in the Superman movies. But in our stories, the crowd would watch while Superhero Hampy overshot the landing point. All heads would turn together as she flew haplessly out of sight.

One time we were out shopping and saw a friend. He started to tell us something just as he stepped onto an escalator. As the moving steps carried him up and away, my son said, in a deadpan voice, 'Superhero Hampy, out to save the day …' It was the kind of in-joke that I think makes family life special. I laughed for days and felt proud of the way my son was able to put the two events together.

As mentioned in the last chapter, our little train character, Tooty, had Magic Dust which allowed him to shrink (and also to grow or fly). We never knew where he got it, but sometimes his supply ran low. It would mysteriously get refilled in the next episode when he needed it. He could use it to become so very small as to be invisible, and sometimes would take trips like in the film *Fantastic Voyage*, where they journey into a human body. He didn't use it in every story, but it came in handy when he needed it. There were also times when his dust got wet or he forgot to fill up his special magic-dust compartment. Sometimes that was very convenient, as for those times when I didn't want him to be able to fly, shrink or grow. Oftentimes the children would suggest that he use it in situations that would have complicated my plot. Those just happened to be the times when there was a problem with the Magic Dust supply.

Tooty could also make his firebox very hot and do things like fill hot-air balloons through his smokestack, evaporate puddles or heat up a damp cave, etc.

And then we had the Magic Tunnel. The Magic Tunnel could not only take characters anywhere, they could also ask it to take them to a specific person. The Magic Tunnel would almost always know where that person was. Occasionally it would not be able to locate someone, but that always turned out to be part of the plot. Sometimes this would be for something like a surprise party, and other times because someone was outside the known universe (usually Hampy – remember, she was 'special' that way). Once, someone in a story created a material that could hide people from The Magic Tunnel. In order to find him, the Magic Tunnel had to search everywhere else in the universe first, using the process of elimination to locate them. Fortunately, the Magic Tunnel can process information very quickly, like a super-computer. In the story, it was heard to say, '"OK, he's not behind this tree, and he's not behind this rock, and he's not down in that dark hole." The Magic Tunnel kept doing that, only billions of times faster. After a few minutes, there was only one place left to look – his bed! You guessed it – the character was in his bed, just like you, closing his eyes for a night of happy dreams ...'

Another problem I ran into was when they suggested a character get help from the Magic Tunnel. Since the Magic Tunnel could go anywhere at any time, it left me vulnerable to always being able to solve tough situations. So sometimes the Magic Tunnel would be on holiday, ill, helping someone else, or 'off in the galaxy where no one can be reached'. I had to get more and more creative as the children got older. They kept coming up with more sophisticated ways to reach the Magic Tunnel, and it really forced me to think outside the box. During the day I would try to come up with ideas that would either be bullet-proof or give the children an opportunity to come up with a loophole. On most occasions they found the loophole I'd left. If they didn't, I would either point it out or wait to discuss it the next day when they were more rested and on top of their game. I found that those scenarios made for very intriguing discussions. This provided great opportunities for my children to learn about physics, astronomy, logic, critical thinking and more. Even when we broke (or shattered) the natural laws of physics, it gave us reasons to discuss how such things would probably never happen in the real world. Playing out fantasy ideas stretches our imagination while providing fertile ground for real learning. Many times I didn't know the answers, and we either looked them up together or the children would ask one of their teachers. In my opinion, one of the most powerful ways to learn is to get curious about something and develop a strong drive to understand it. Of course, once they did, they would explain to me how some of the things I had happen in the story couldn't work. When that happened, I found a way out: magic!

## Magic

> Any sufficiently advanced technology
> is indistinguishable from magic.
>
> **ARTHUR C. CLARKE**

Be careful with assigning magical powers. These are different from super powers. Once you open the door to magic, you open up a Pandora's Box of endless possibilities. Magic can be used to do virtually anything, getting the characters out of tight spaces where you and your child could instead be using higher levels of creativity or logical thinking. Magic can definitely be too easy a way out.

Once I tried using it, I realized the problem: my children kept going back to it to solve any dilemma that came up. 'Why don't they just use magic and make the giant evil armadillo go away?' I finally had to put a stop to it. One of the characters set off an anti-magic device that spread across the entire universe and all the other universes we'd created up to that point. Since the device was magical in itself, it could also keep any future universes from having magic. Therefore it remained the only device of its kind and the only source of magic there could be. Finally, I had put an end to it. Or so I thought! Later the children suggested that the characters use the Magic Tunnel to go back in time and keep the anti-magic device from being activated. As Homer Simpson would say, 'D'oh!'

So, I had to change the original formula to include stopping any magic that happened in the past as well. For some reason I didn't think of that when I came up with the device. Now that I think back on some of these episodes, one of the things I liked the best was the challenge of coming up with solutions to the ingenuity of my children.

> It is good to rub and polish our brain
> against that of others.
>
> **MICHEL DE MONTAIGNE**

With the prevalence of Harry Potter in our lives, the concept of magic is well known to our children. You may want to consider leaving magic out of your stories altogether. Since 'real magic' isn't real anyway, you can certainly insist or suggest that magic belongs in the world of Harry Potter but not in our bedtime stories. If you want your children to be good at solving the problems that life will throw their way, then consider that they will have to do it without magic. Getting them to do critical thinking in a fun, safe way prepares them for the real world in a gentle, loving manner.

## Time Travel

Learning is a treasure that will follow its owner everywhere.

**CHINESE PROVERB**

This concept can be a lot of fun. You can have your characters go back in time to interact with famous people and places. We always used the Magic Tunnel when they felt the need. You can get back in time any way you like in your own stories. This is where creativity comes in. There could be a special liquid that they squirt on an object to turn it into a time machine, or it can happen going through a car wash or your tumble dryer. It doesn't matter. It could be different every time. As long as you come up with it together, it will be fun. Your characters can go back in time to meet people who can help them solve problems today.

We went back and had adventures with Benjamin Franklin and his kite, one of our characters talked with Winston Churchill about fear, and Winnie the Worm got stuck in Napoleon's shirt (so in all those pictures of him with his hand in his shirt front, he's actually just reaching in there to get her out). This gives you the opportunity to talk about famous events and places. You can do a quick information search online and weave a fact or two into the story, making it educational as well as fun. The next day you can talk further about it, deepening their understanding of important people, times and places. Sometimes I would do that in the car on the way to school. 'Hey, remember last night when Hampy was helping to design the first pyramid? I learned that one of the reasons they have four sides is that it's the best shape to cheat the wind. With all the sand blowing around, a square building would not have lasted as long.'

The idea is to learn something yourself, then find a way to make it fun for your child to learn about. This not only teaches them something worth knowing, it demonstrates that learning is a lifelong process. I often have both children and adults in my SuperReading course. I believe it's good to have children seeing adults continuing to learn. It will help them to keep ahead of the game when they get older. I'm sure that the saying, 'You have to learn more to earn more' will be equally true a few decades from now. So will the phrase, 'Readers are Leaders.'

To teach is to learn twice.

**JOSEPH JOUBERT**

# Teaching Time-Management

# Teaching
# Time-management

Nothing is ours except time.

**MARCUS SENECA**

Children can learn to budget their time. Sometimes my children would bargain to watch a TV programme and do their homework later. If recording it on the VCR wasn't an option, they had that choice. However, they were also reminded of when bedtime would be, so if they did not finish their homework on time there would be no bedtime story and no grumbling about it. If they followed those rules without complaining, sometimes I would sneak in and tell them an abbreviated story to reward them for such good behaviour. I'd make a point of saying that I could not do this every time, so they wouldn't come to depend on it. While it did not happen that often, my strategy was to reward them when they had been particularly well behaved during the rest of the day as well. I would point this out to them, as well as pointing out the consequences of when their behaviour was not up to par. After a while it began to sink in that there are often consequences for acceptable and unacceptable behaviour. When there were minor scuffles, they would get a shorter story.

If your children have chores, homework or other responsibilities to complete before their story, be sure they have plenty of warning to finish up on time. My suggestion is that they get several announcements of the time so they can pace themselves. It's really easy for children to lose track of the time, especially when they are either tired or excited about something. Time is more of an adult concept, and I believe it's up to parents to help children be time-sensitive without making them time-paranoid. Time can be our friend if we learn to be aware of it. However, it's definitely a learned skill. Awareness of time is also more of a left-brained skill. The most creative, right-brained people are usually rubbish at keeping track of time. Babies only know when they are hungry, tired or wet. And most of that is fairly independent of time anyway. They are simply not aware of time. Learning to grasp how long 10 minutes is takes practice. What I'm saying is to help your child with gentle reminders that time is passing. You might want to time them when they do a good job of brushing and flossing. Perhaps that takes 5 minutes to complete. If they need to shower or bathe, that takes time, too. If the whole process takes 22 minutes, be sure that the other responsibilities are completed with enough time for personal hygiene and into bed for their story at the decided time. If your children say prayers, decide whether they do them before or after the story (I recommend before. They can pray for a great plot!). If they have a drink of water, it definitely needs to be done before the story begins.

You may delay, but time will not.

**BENJAMIN FRANKLIN**

I believe it is your job, as the adults, to watch the clock. Fair warning of deadlines, based on previous experience, provides your children with the opportunity to be responsible people. If they mess around, they lose the privilege of getting a story. Just make sure they understand these consequences before you ever deny a story. They need to understand exactly what the agreement is, appropriate for their age and development.

The storytelling itself needs to have a flexible time limit. In bed by, say, 8.30 p.m., story done by 8.45 or so. It's up to the child to learn to start the washing process when they are told, otherwise the story will have to be shorter. In plain language, they have to *manage their time* to get the maximum storytelling experience, because around 8.45 the story will be wrapped up whether it was 15 minutes or 2 minutes long.

Having said this, I'd suggest being flexible for any of the following reasons: the story is particularly great and needs a little more time; there was no hot water, causing a delay; a special guest stayed later than expected; or anything beyond the child's control that delays the routine or rituals. The child should not be punished for circumstances created by either the adults or nature! They can sometimes be given a choice between continuing an activity and a shorter story. Whatever choice they make, stick to it. They have to learn the consequences of their decisions.

A man who gives his children habits of industry
provides for them better than by giving them fortune.

**RICHARD WHATELY**

## Bedtime Will Be Better

Putting time-management skills to work will make you feel
better about bedtime, too! Most parents dread bedtime as
much as their children. In talking with other parents I've
realized that most of them have no real plan for bedtime.
They put off thinking about it or doing anything about it
just as much as their children do. They are aware when it's
approaching, but have no plan or ritual other than giving
orders to wash and brush teeth, get undressed, etc. They see it
as an impending battle of wills that leaves them feeling weary,
guilty, frustrated and angry. Once you establish storytelling
as part of a nightly routine, you will (mostly) look forward to
the ritual because of the bonding, fun and pleasant surprises
in store. I will admit that once in a while I was so tired that it
seemed like it would be a chore. However, once we got into
the story I was always glad we had. The stories got me smiling
and often left me with far more energy than when I began.
It got to the point that bedtime was fun and all I had to do
was suggest it was time and the children were off to brush
their teeth. The handful of times they asked to wait (without
a legitimate reason) I simply said I would begin telling the
story in 10 minutes whether they were there or not. They
knew I would be able to tell if they did an adequate job
washing, so there was no cutting corners.

The routine of a bedtime story will make your evenings far
more pleasant and less stressful. I'm not claiming it will
always be a bed of roses. It will be a tool that provides a

strategy for making your lives better. The more you use it, the better it will serve you.

The best portion of a good man's life is his little, nameless, unremembered acts of kindness and of love.

**WILLIAM WORDSWORTH**

# THE 'GOOD NIGHT' PART

# The 'Good Night' Part

There are several places you can be when telling the story. You can be in bed with your child, lying down, all cosy. You can be on the bed sitting up, with the child either lying down or sitting up as well. You can be in a chair next to the bed, with the child either lying down or sitting up. You can be standing with the child either lying down or sitting up. For the most part I don't think there's any right or wrong. I do think, however, that there are advantages and disadvantages to each option.

I've tried all the possibilities. What I found worked for me most of the time was me sitting next to the bed (or sometimes on the edge of the bed). The reasons had to do with convenience. I talk with my hands. Although snuggling up close was fun, it made it hard for me to think and communicate effectively. Another problem in lying next to my child was that sometimes at the end they grabbed onto me and would not let go. That made the smooth transition to sleep problematic. Sometimes I needed to get up and act out what was going on. If I was lying down, especially beneath the covers, it was too disturbing to the process. Another problem

I had with lying down was that it caused me to start falling asleep myself! My mind would begin drifting and I would lose the thread of the story. The time my daughter reminds me of was when I was talking about our little train lost in a silver mine. I closed my eyes, mumbled a few incoherent words, and said, 'And then a circus went by.' My daughter shook me and demanded to know where the circus had come from! I barely remembered saying it. She said, 'Dad – you were falling asleep!' 'Oh, sorry, I …' 'Wake up, you're doing it again!' Lying down was just too tempting. The only way I could possibly finish was to stand and come up with something. I learned my lesson. I could sit on the bed, but if I was really exhausted, I needed to either sit in a chair or stand. All I can say is that at least I didn't start snoring!

Another consideration is your physical health. Your child's mattress may not be suited to your back. If the bed is small it's possible to fall off. Again, unfortunately, I am speaking from personal experience. You need to find your own best style. I would suggest pulling up a chair to begin with. I believe it will add to your creativity. If later you want to get more snuggle time in, you can try lying down. While some studies have shown that most people are more creative while standing (thinking on your feet), it just doesn't feel right for a bedtime story. In my mind, someone telling a bedtime story is sitting next to the bed. Standing makes it look like you can't wait to leave. The only other reason to stand, temporarily, is to illustrate something happening in the plot, like a giant attacking a fortress. Another little ploy I used was to sit in a chair, then as I finished up I would lean over to give a kiss, standing up afterward. Then I would either push the chair out of the way or remove it from the room as I exited. It was like a smooth ballet. One thing just naturally led to the next, and finally, to freedom! Just kidding. Really. I'm kidding!

The final act occurs when you bring the story to a close and administer the traditional good-night kiss. A warm, loving hug is always nice as well. I would usually tell them I love them and that I would see them in the morning. I would blow a final kiss as I turned down the light and closed the door.

The most important thing about the final 'Good night' is that it is in fact final. Unless your child starts throwing up or there's a fire (may it never happen!), that last kiss you blow to them is your exit. If they try going for a glass of water or something, remind them of the rules. It's unfair for them to break those rules. This goes for you too: if you break the rules, it teaches them that you do not mean what you say. And all your preparation, diligence and loving effort would now be diminished. Not lost, by any means, just less than they should be. Once you close their door, or turn down the light, it should be your turn to have time for whatever you want (or need) to do as an adult.

My advice is to be firm but flexible in case of a true emergency. If the child is really feeling ill or having some other problem, you want to make sure they are safe and feel loved. There will be times when it's a tough call. Just make sure they feel totally loved when all is said and done. There were a few times one of mine would start coughing while we were laughing. She really did need another little drink afterwards. I went and got it, so she remained in bed. She sat up, took her time drinking it, stretching it out, and then lay back down. I administered another kiss and told her I loved her and would see her in the morning. All was well.

# EXCEPTIONS TO THE RULES

# Exceptions to the Rules

If you obey all the rules, you miss all the fun.

**KATHARINE HEPBURN**

Occasionally it might be really late and you want to tell a great story you thought of during the day. Even though it is past bedtime, I say go for it. If you are 'given' a great story, it's probably meant to be used now. A few extra minutes will not bring the universe crashing to an end. As William Somerset Maugham said, 'Excess on occasion is exhilarating. It prevents moderation from acquiring the deadening effect of a habit.'

So, every month or two, make a big deal of staying up a little past bedtime. Just make sure that the next night you get right back into the routine. That makes it special – not expected. Those are the warm fuzzy memories that will stay with them a long time – when you broke the rules together. However, doing it too much ruins the effect. It would be like eating ice-cream every day. OK, bad example, but you know what I mean.

Another possibility is not telling a story one night. Sometimes parents go out, and they leave too early to tell a story before they go. If they are going to a play or a film, there may be no convenient time to call in. In that case, I would issue a rain check for a big story the next night to make up for it. I would also suggest they make one up themselves and tell me about it the next day. In either event, make sure you get right back into the ritual the next day. The leverage gained by getting them into bed with good feelings is far too important to let it slide.

Another exception would be when your child tells you they don't want a story. An alternative that will keep the ritual going is to tell them an interesting account from your past. This can be anything from any part of your life. I would certainly keep it appropriate to your child's level of development. For example, I would leave out the one about the drinking binge at the fraternity house. Perhaps you could share the one when you got lost in the woods for two hours following a yellow-bellied sapsucker. These stories can give your child a good idea of who you are. It's fun to relate stories about you and your own parents. This was important for us, as we lived thousands of miles from the grandparents. According to my daughter, my life accounts gave her good insight into the person I am. I hope that was a good thing ...

> The stories that you tell about your
> past shape your future.
>
> **ERIC RANSDELL**

# DREAMING

# Dreaming

I dream my painting, and then I paint my dream.

**VINCENT VAN GOGH**

Some scientists believe that one function of dreaming is for the brain to make sense of the day. Even though dreams are often bizarre and seemingly devoid of logic, who is to say this is not part of the process? The fact that completely weird events seem totally normal to the dreamer suggests to me that the theory is true. Our brain has no problem seeing impossible scenarios as perfectly normal. By the time morning arrives, the brain has gone over all those events and has experienced them as OK, unhampered by our conscious mind. It may not be the entire explanation behind dreams, but it may explain part of their function. Therefore a story before bedtime that brings some of the day's events into focus might help to start the process going. By starting the process with positive thoughts, the night's dreams could be happier and lead to a more restful sleep.

One possible reason for nightmares is that the brain is dealing with scary information which it cannot process in any other way. Talking about events and feelings in a loving environment usually has a calming effect, and is certainly better than keeping those kinds of feelings locked up inside. When we feel alone and misunderstood, our fears can grow and get the better of us. I'm not saying that bedtime stories alone can eliminate nightmares or fears. I'm saying that doing what we can to help is no bad thing.

As a general rule, try to make your stories end on a happy note; especially with small children. The idea is to entertain, share, and try to resolve any issues that may have come up during the day.

Sleep time is also a good time for creativity. We are never too young to begin problem solving. We can learn to programme our mind to consider problems and work on solutions while we sleep. Often we will then wake up and have an answer there in our conscious mind. The process is simple and straightforward. In the last few minutes before we are likely to fall asleep, we can give our mind a positive command to give us a solution. We can also visualize ourselves waking up with that solution. We can say to ourselves that we are going to wake up with a solution to 'Problem X'. This would sound something like, 'Brain, I want you to work on solving the problem with that bully at school. When I wake up, please have a great answer for me. Thank you.' Then imagine opening your eyes in the morning and smiling at the idea you are having to make things better.

This will work, especially if the technique is practised consistently. The human mind likes to solve problems. In fact, it cannot help but try to answer any question it has been asked. You can help children to understand this concept. If they have seen the film *Roger Rabbit*, they will know that the 'Toons' cannot help themselves when they hear a certain rhythm. Do you know which one I mean? It has seven beats, that go da da da DA da, da DA. If a Toon hears the first five knocks, they are compelled to finish with the last two (da DA!), as Roger Rabbit must do. By telling your child that their brain will want to find an answer in the same way, it will make this sound like fun and teach them the valuable lesson of persistence.

> Persistent people begin their success where others end in failures.
>
> **EDWARD EGGLESTON**

Many people believe that persistence and resilience are the two most important traits a person can have when it comes to personal achievement. Most people give up on themselves far too soon in their endeavours. They get discouraged if things don't work out quickly. Patience is usually a learned virtue. In today's world of fast food, fast electronic games and flashing imagery on television, it's valuable to learn about slowing down. Since this is a book about creating bedtime stories, it's natural that learning to slow down at the end of the day is important. In school it's important to be patient and persistent when learning difficult subjects. I've heard so many children claim how they are rubbish at maths or some other subject. The lesson of patience is an important one in these cases. After all, Rome wasn't built in a day. Most valuable skills take time to master, or even to become somewhat competent at. Children look first to their parents to learn how to react to failure.

Eventually you will hear your words pouring from your child's mouth. If they see you taking setbacks in your stride, they will probably model that behaviour. If they see you getting frustrated and down on yourself, they will learn to give up too easily. We have only a few years where our children model us. Once they become teenagers (or near to being) the opposite may be true. They may start to rebel. The early years, especially the first eight years, are when patterns are set. After that, learning basic life-lessons becomes increasingly difficult.

Having children gives us the opportunity to revisit our character and be better people for their sake. Of course, that's the theory. The reality is that often our children stress us more than anything, and we're lucky to get through the day without pulling all our hair out. That said, if even once a day we can be our better selves to provide that model of patience, everyone benefits.

Let me tell you the secret that has led me to my goal. My strength lies solely in my tenacity.

**LOUIS PASTEUR**

# STARTING YOUR STORY

# Starting Your Story

The beginning is the most important part of the work.

**PLATO**

My children liked every story to start with the same opening words. This gave a sense of ritual, familiarity and anticipation. Often I would do variations on a theme with the opening. Our standard opening was, 'One day, Tooty the Train was huffing and puffing along the tracks.' Depending on the mood I would add other verbs: 'One day, Tooty the Train was huffing and puffing and chiffing and chuffing along the tracks.' Once in a while, if the children were particularly silly (or I wanted to encourage them to be), I would continue with, 'and sniffing and snuffing and chirping and burping' and on and on until they begged for mercy. Some of the words made sense, others most certainly did not. Then the story would really start, usually with, 'All of a sudden, Tooty heard a strange sound' or 'saw something he had never seen before' or 'felt something land on him', or something else out of the ordinary.

Usually it was one of the characters we'd developed, coming to him for help. It could be an old familiar one or someone new. The problem usually required Tooty to travel to some far-off location. As time went on, Tooty needed faster ways of getting places, so I invented his Magic Dust and the Magic Tunnel.

If the Magic Tunnel was taking the characters to another planet, I always created a planet that had some very strange attributes. Here is a partial list of the planets my children and I have created: the Square Planet, the Flat Planet, the Biscuit Planet, the Planet where the Water Is Black (or any other colour you like), the Backwards Planet (where everyone walks backwards), the Singing Planet (where people communicate in song), the Rhyming Planet (where they speak in rhyme), the Train Planet (where only trains live and the tracks go everywhere), the Rainy Planet (where it rains 24/7), the Ocean Planet (all water), and the Planet that Can't Be Found.

> How wonderful it is that nobody need wait a single moment before starting to improve the world.
>
> **ANNE FRANK**

Starting a story off with the same words each time signals an official start of the ritual. While most children love to be creative and hear creative stories, most also like them to begin the same way. There is a feeling of security and anticipation when your stories always begin the same way. You will often see an adorably mischievous look on your child's face as the story begins and they settle in for the experience. They know that soon the two of you will be taking off on yet another great adventure with his or her favourite characters. The opening sentence is like two pilots going over their flight checklist.

That part of the routine is always the same. The route and destination, though, can be vastly different each time.

Let's look at some possible ways to begin your stories. Let's use Tappy this time.

'Once upon a time, there was a very special tap shoe named Tappy.'

'A long time ago, in a dance studio far, far away …'

'Snuggle into your blankets and I will tell you an amazing tale of Tappy the Tap Shoe.'

'One day, Tappy the Tap Shoe was clipping and clopping along the floor, when suddenly …'

'It is time. Time to tell all who dare to hear the touching tale of Tappy the Tap Shoe.'

'Lie back and relax. We will tell your bedtime story. We will control the voices you hear and the characters you see. For the next few minutes open your mind and enjoy the adventures of … Tappy the Tap Shoe.'

'Come one, come all … Open your ears and open your mind … And I will tell you a tale.'

You can make one up and try it out. Your children will soon let you know what they like. Again, you need to be flexible and open. Try a few different beginnings. Your child may want a different one each time, though I'm guessing that would be unusual. For the sake of ritual, I strongly suggest using the same line to begin each story. The purpose is to signal the beginning of the story with firm certainty.

### Tooty and the Trapped Squirrel

One day, Tooty the Train was huffing and puffing along the tracks, when all of a sudden he heard a familiar sound. It was his good friend, Mr Woodpecker. He was hammering away on a nearby tree (tap tap tap). Tooty stopped, got off the tracks and went over to visit with his good friend. Tooty looked up at him, amazed at how hard his friend could hit the tree with his bill. 'You must be pretty hungry today!' said Tooty. Mr Woodpecker was so busy he didn't even hear Tooty. So Tooty heated up his firebox and let out a short blast on his whistle. Mr Woodpecker looked around. He was about to get back to his pecking when he looked down towards the ground. There was Tooty smiling up at him. 'Good morning to you,' said Mr Woodpecker. Tooty asked again how hungry his friend was. Mr Woodpecker looked confused for a moment, and then flew down to Tooty. 'I'm not very hungry at all, Tooty. I'm on a special assignment!' Now it was Tooty's turn to look confused. 'What kind of assignment?' 'Well, there's a baby squirrel trapped in the trunk of this tree. I made an air hole so he could breathe better. If I work hard enough, I may be able to make the hole big enough for the little fellow to climb out.' Tooty was impressed. 'Is there anything I can do to help?' Mr Woodpecker thought about it, and asked Tooty if he could heat up his firebox and blast some steam on the hole. If it softened up a bit, then Mr Woodpecker's work would be easier.

So Tooty got himself all fired up while Mr Woodpecker flew him up to the hole. They told Sonny the Squirrel to scrunch down, and Tooty let out a big blast of steam right on the hole. Sure enough, it made the woodpecker's work much easier, and in no time at all little Sonny was scrambling out of the hole. Sonny gave Mr Woodpecker and Tooty big hugs, and then ran off to nuzzle with his mother and father. A few seconds later, Sonny was happily playing and chasing with the other little squirrels again.

To celebrate their success, Mr Woodpecker and Tooty were treated to lunch by Sonny's parents. Tooty had 30-weight oil with a glass of water, and Mr Woodpecker had a plate of roasted grubs. Just as they were finishing, Lenny Llama came running into the restaurant. He told Tooty that a group of hikers were trapped in a cave, and they needed Tooty's help to get them out. Tooty excused himself from the table and went outside. He got out some of his special Magic Dust, sprinkled some on, and out came his wings. Before you could say Poof, he was airborne and rocketing away toward the old caves. Tomorrow we'll see how Tooty rescues the hikers from certain waiting. Meanwhile, the hikers were tired, so they took out their pads and blankets, and decided to take a nap. Soon, just like you, they drifted off into a peaceful sleep, knowing that Tooty the Train was on his way, and they would all be safe soon enough. The end.

# MIDDLES AND ENDINGS

# Middles and Endings

Motivation is what gets you started.
Habit is what keeps you going.

**JIM RYUH**

Once you have the story begun, there are several ways to proceed. You can do it all solo, or you can encourage the children to participate. If they don't want to contribute directly to the plot, there is another way for them. You can leave a word out which they can fill in. You can begin this technique with rather obvious answers that are easy for them. Here are some examples:

'When Scruffy fell in the lake, his fur got all _____.'

'Jingles walked straight up to the horse and fed him a cube of _____.'

'When they got to the orchard, Penelope reached up into the tree and picked herself a nice big, red, juicy _____.'

'When their order of chips finally arrived, Flippy could not believe it. Once again they'd remembered the vinegar, but they forgot to sprinkle on the _____.'

You know what your child is likely to know. There are certain things that would be obvious to adults but not to children. Make sure they are successful every time they guess an answer. Over time you can make the missing words a bit more difficult. After a while you can have them fill in words that will affect the plot. Before long they will be making suggestions left, right and centre. This will build their confidence. If they give an answer that makes no sense, be gentle about correcting them. Depending on their age, you may want to ignore it completely. Or you can tell them how clever they are to suggest such a word there.

I remember an incident with my daughter when she was about eight or nine years old. We were playing a guessing game, though I think the similarity is close enough. OK, it's a funny story and I really want to share it with you! We were going through the alphabet and giving clues to words that begin with the letter we had reached. It was my turn to use the letter 'S'. The word I thought of was 'sip'. My clue was, 'This is how you drink a really fine wine.' Her answer had me laughing for days. She replied, 'With a straw?' For an eight-year-old that made perfect sense. And although I may not be the world's expert on wine, I know you don't use a straw. The point is that I told her what a great guess she had made. Then I told her that the word I was thinking of was 'sip'. I explained how wine is a drink that adults like to savour. They really take their time with it. They take little sips and slowly enjoy the flavour, as opposed to gulping it down all at once.

## Ending a Story

> Though no one can go back and make a
> brand-new start, anyone can start from now
> and make a brand-new ending.

**CARL BARD**

You can have an 'official' ending line to your stories – or maybe two: one that wraps it up or one for continuing the next night (a 'cliffhanger'). A cliffhanger dates from the early days of cinema where the hero would literally be hanging from a cliff when the film would end. The conclusion of this short film could be seen later alongside another feature film. It was a precursor to TV shows with continuing plots. The suspense kept audiences coming back to see how their hero survived the situation. You can accomplish the same thing. Give your child something special to look forward to the next night. A wonderful time to do this is when you know that tomorrow night will need special handling. Perhaps there is a party for adults and the children would dearly love to participate. The adults need their own time and you will have extra pull if you set up a cliffhanger the night before. Their curiosity can overcome their desire to crash the party.

Another time to use a cliffhanger is when you develop a particularly intriguing story line. Every once in a while you will hit upon an especially great plot or situation. When that happens, you'll want to 'milk it' for all it's worth! Stretch it out a bit. Not only will it provide an extra night or two of story line, it will give you time during the day to think about where it might go. I've had some of these last for a whole week. You will come up with ideas that lend themselves to variations on a theme. One example was the Biscuit Planet.

It was relatively thin, so people could burrow through to the other side. The first night the characters discovered people living on the other side. The second night they all went through to say hello. However, at the same time, the people from the other side had had the same idea. So they'd simply switched sides of the planet! The third night they made so many holes that their planet was in danger of breaking into pieces. The fourth night the planet broke in half, and was then in danger of drifting apart. The fifth night they contacted the Jam Planet and bought enough jam to make a Sandwich Planet. Now there was only half the area, so they baked more land. It could have gone on and on. Some of the ideas were mine and some were from my children.

When your children get old enough, you can have discussions about how such things could not really work (gravity, atmosphere, temperatures, etc.). It becomes a great lesson in the difference between fantasy and what we know as reality.

> Reality is but a work in progress waiting
> to be shaped by a creative mind.
>
> **JIM SHOOTER**

It's fun to create different plots and places. It's also fun to learn about what science teaches us about what is likely to be possible. Remember that much of what was fantasy 100 or 150 years ago is reality today. Creativity is the catalyst for productive progress.

By exposing your children to seemingly impossible ideas, you can stretch their imagination to the point where they may solve problems that others would not even attempt because they see them as impossible.

To the timid and hesitating everything is
impossible because it seems so.

**SIR WALTER SCOTT**


The young do not know enough to be prudent,
and therefore they attempt the impossible – and
achieve it, generation after generation.

**PEARL S. BUCK**

# Children's Emotions, Parents' Emotions

# Children's Emotions, Parents' Emotions

The best inheritance a parent can give his children
is a few minutes of his time each day.

**O. A. BATTISTA**

I'd like to suggest that you keep your stories positive. If something bad happens in life, use your judgement about having the characters deal with it. Whatever they do should be supportive and constructive. Take your lead from your child. If they want to deal with it, OK. If they just want a regular episode that ignores what has happened, go with it. They may not want to contaminate their characters with real-life tragedy. They may need to escape completely. Proceed gently. No forcing. Give it time. If they do want the characters to deal with it, they may want this to be over a few days or weeks. If they want it they will let you know when it's time.

Most children live with emotionally wounded parents. Virtually everyone on Earth has been wounded in some way, some more than others. Most of the serious wounding happens when we are children. Therefore it would seem prudent to be sensitive to wounds that our children sustain. Dealing with emotions is always tricky. While this is not a child-rearing book *per se*, I do want to share a thought or two on the subject.

Emotions are neurochemical events that occur in our brain. One thing that turns them into destructive patterns is the way we deal with them. If we dwell on them, we give them power. If we are forced to dwell on them it gives them more power. I believe there is a middle ground.

The first step is to acknowledge the way we feel. Once those chemicals are released and we feel a specific way, that feeling is true and real. Denying it or mislabelling it does not alter its truthfulness. In fact, it causes confusion and inner turmoil. If your child is feeling sad, acknowledge it and be there for them. Ask what happened and agree that sadness is the appropriate way to feel. 'Oh, that was bad. I feel bad just hearing about it. I'd be feeling sad just like you are.' It must be true, because their brain released the chemicals that caused them to experience sadness. The big question is what to do next. I would suggest experiencing the sadness together. Talk it over and compare notes. Empathize with your child. This will teach them that they correctly identified the emotion they felt. Sharing this will usually help them to feel better. Then demonstrate that once they have spent an appropriate amount of time feeling sad, they can return to a state of happiness again. Teach them that what we focus on can determine how we feel. When they want to feel happy again, they should focus on things that make them happy. Then their brain will release the chemicals that cause happy feelings.

Life is not about being in a constant state of joy. Life is about appropriately experiencing many situations and emotions. After a few days we would get bored and no longer appreciate a state of joy anyway. Life is about learning to accept that we have emotions, and learning to deal well with them. Once we do, it's time to get on with things and leave it behind.

> Shared joy is a double joy; shared sorrow
> is half a sorrow.
>
> **SWEDISH PROVERB**

The other important lesson about emotions is that they are all related. They are all chemical events. I also believe that some of these chemical events have a spiritual element to them. If we try to shut down certain emotions, the effect spills over to other emotions. By denying 'negative' emotions, we learn to not believe ourselves. When we are feeling sad (a true condition) and an adult tells us we have no reason to be sad, or no right to be sad, we can believe there is something wrong with us. At that point, we just suppress emotions so we do not have to look at this faulty thing called 'me'. If we feel that we cannot be trusted to recognize our emotions, we can start to doubt our ability to have any emotions. People like this have great difficulty loving others and themselves, because they think it's all an illusion that cannot be trusted. That causes pain. Pain is avoided by most people. Their solution is to not feel anything. As a result, their brain becomes less adept at providing the chemicals, and their cells become less adept at receiving the chemicals. The final outcome is an adult who is half-dead inside. They may keep very busy to avoid having to feel anything other than physical accomplishment, but that's a high price to pay for productivity. One solution is to acknowledge what is real and then move on to something else that is real. Emotions are real, and they exist with or without your permission or understanding.

Here's a possible scenario that may help. A child sits in a chair, looking sad.

**Parent:** 'Hi.'

**Child:** *'Hi.'*

**Parent:** 'You look like I do when I'm sad. Are you feeling sad?' (Observation)

**Child:** *'Yes.'*

**Parent:** 'Can I ask what happened?'

**Child:** *'Tommy said he wasn't my friend any more.'*

**Parent:** 'Hmmm. That would make me sad too.'

**Child:** *'Yeah.'*

**Parent:** 'When that happened to me, I felt like someone kicked me in my stomach.'

**Child:** *'That happened to you?'*

**Parent:** 'Yes, it did.'

**Child:** *'When you were a child?'*

**Parent:** 'Yes. My best friend got angry with me, and said I could never play with his toys ever again. He said he hated me. I felt angry at first, then very sad. I felt like crying.'

**Child:** *'Me too.'*

**Parent:** 'I can see that. You look upset. I would be worried if you didn't.'

**Child:** *'Why?'*

**Parent:** 'That would mean you didn't care about having friends. When we lose one, even for a while, it hurts and we feel sad.'

**Child:** *'What do you mean, "For a while"?'*

**Parent:** 'In a day or two, you'll probably make up and be friends again. Or you might not. If you do, you'll feel happy again. If not, you'll be sad a little longer, and then find another friend.'

**Child:** *'What if I don't find another friend?'*

**Parent:** 'Then you'll either be sad, or you'll find some way to be happy.'

**Child:** *'How would I be happy?'*

**Parent:** 'Well, you still have me (and your mother, siblings, etc.). I can be a pretty good friend.' (soft punch on the arm or a tickle)

**Child:** *'I guess so. We have fun together, don't we?'*

**Parent:** 'Yes, we do. Hey – I have a feeling ...'

**Child:** *'What is it?'*

**Parent:** 'I have a feeling that, before you know it, you'll be playing and having fun again. You want to bet?'

**Child:** *'Sure. What's the bet?'*

**Parent:** 'Two hugs and a big kiss.'

**Child:** *'OK.'*

**Parent:** 'We have to ante up, so let's have one hug right now. (HUG) That was good. If you could play any game right now, with me, what would it be?'

**Child:** *(gives an answer)*

**Parent:**  'Great! I'll get a pack of cards (or whatever).
          You clear the table. Let's see who's fastest!'

**Child:**   'OK – go!'

By this point, a number of things have happened. The child's emotional state was acknowledged, giving them the feedback that they are normal and have successfully understood their emotion. This means they are not the only person in history to ever feel this way, and they can survive it. You showed interest, then understanding. You also did not vilify the friend, who is also only human. Your job is not to add fuel to the fire, just to empathize and identify. Then you gave an example to show you understand. Next you planted a seed that they would probably be playing again soon. You also acknowledged that if that didn't happen, life would go on and be OK. You also hinted that being happy is a choice. Next, you assured your child that they are still loved and have other people who will stand by them. After that, it's time to gently move on. There's no sense in wallowing in negative feelings.

By changing where we focus our attention, we can now look for more positive emotions. You supplied the opportunity by suggesting that you two play a game. While playing, you can either turn the discussion to something else entirely, or talk more about the situation or about emotions. I'm not going to make any suggestions at this point. The rest is up to you. If the child wants to speak about it, follow the same basic format. Acknowledge their emotion, let them know it's normal, then teach them how to move on when they want to feel happy again. You can talk about human foibles and how most people find clever ways to screw up the best things. Anyone can be forgiven, and friends are something you try to keep. Every once in a while we become friends with a destructive person. When that happens, we need to find someone else to call our friend. Sometimes it's tough, but that's life too. Friendship is always an option.

*We cherish our friends not for their ability to amuse us, but for ours to amuse them.*

**EVELYN WAUGH**

The bottom line is to respect your child's emotions. If you do not, you will pay a heavy price later on. I would suggest that you respect your own emotions as well. They are as real as it gets. This is who we are and how we work. To ignore that is foolish. We like to think of ourselves as rational beings. We are that as well. I have come to the belief that we are primarily emotional beings, however. In stressful situations, we tend to react from emotions first. The first step to getting a handle on that is to correctly identify what is happening. If you remain ignorant or stubborn about it, you will continue to fall victim to it. Worse, you will pass that fate on to your children.

*Be slow in choosing a friend, slower in changing.*

**BENJAMIN FRANKLIN**

Your characters can use positive techniques to control their emotions from time to time. One way is to alter the object of their focus. When we lose something, most of us focus on the lost item and on how we will suffer because it is gone. A more useful tactic is to focus on the good things we still have, or to figure out how we can replace what we've lost, or to ask ourselves how we might be better off without it. Your characters can be thankful for the good things they have, even when something they really enjoyed having is taken away. You can also have them pull together and set about replacing the item if was of vital importance. Either way, their speech and actions should reflect solid resolve to let go of the original item, especially if it was replaceable. For example, you could have a character in a story say, 'That was my favourite football. I'll never have another one that means so much to me! WAAAH!'

Or you can try this instead: 'I lost my football and I really like playing football. How can I get another one so we can play together?'

The second way acknowledges the loss, but then moves immediately into positive action. What a great lesson for children (and adults) to learn. Having your characters model that behaviour is a beautiful way to illustrate the lesson.

## Parents' Emotions

Cherish your emotions and never undervalue them.

**ROBERT HENRI**

Many emotional states are learned. I'm sure some authorities would say that *all* emotions are learned, or at least reinforced. As adults we like to think that we have some level of mastery over our emotions. While it is true that we have more practice than our children, we must recognize that our emotional patterns were developed in childhood and reinforced through adolescence and adulthood. What does that mean? It means that we can all still react like when we were children. It also means that we can relearn to control our emotional states. And it means we can easily pass on our emotional shortcomings to our children.

I went to a seminar where the person leading it referred to children as 'parentologists'. He told us that our children study us, looking for (and usually exploiting) our hot buttons. They work us over looking for weaknesses, then exploit them as best they can. Most children will find out through trial and error how far they can push us. At that threshold, some children will back off; others will try to blast past it to some unknown level. If you have children, it's not hard to figure out which variety you have!

One reason our children can push our buttons is that we see them as a reflection of us.

> Few things are harder to put up with than
> the annoyance of a good example.
>
> **MARK TWAIN**

There are few things as devastating as having our weaknesses paraded about in public for all to see. It doesn't matter too much whether it's in front of someone we know or a group of strangers. It still pushes raw nerves right to the bone. Having it all displayed in private isn't all that much better. In private, at least there's a chance nobody else will find out. The problem is, of course, that in private we're more likely to say and do things we'll regret even more.

Why am I devoting a section to this? At the end of a long day we are at our most vulnerable. We are tired, we have beaten off the cold cruel world as best we can, and we have sought the refuge of the cave. Now we are safe; no more attacks. Now all that is left is to bask in the loving warmth and glowing admiration of our children. Yeah – right! If only that scenario were the case. It may be true, at least for a while.

However, at bedtime it can all come crashing down. By that time everyone has been tossed around by the world out there, and they all want some loving attention. The question is, how much more do we have to give? The answer is that we have more than enough, if the environment is set up properly. By environment, I mean both the external and internal. The external we talked about before: tooth brushing and washing. The internal is where we visualize the upcoming scenario with love and patience. We have an agreed-to plan and we follow it through. Everyone gets what they expect. If they do not get 100 per cent of it tonight, they know that the plan is to do better the next night. Sometimes life is a series of compromises. As long as everyone's heart is in the right place, it can work out in the long term. The important thing to remember, for all concerned, is that every night each person in the family will do all they are capable of doing to make the bedtime plan work that night.

From time to time you may have to remind your children that you have needs too. To function well, adults need downtime at the end of the day. Someday your children will have children, and they will need special adult time too. This is the way of things. Life moves in an endless cycle. Just show them that part in *The Lion King* where Mufasa explains the Circle of Life to Simba. They'll get it!

> If I could wish for my life to be perfect, it would be tempting but I would have to decline, for life would no longer teach me anything.
>
> **ALLYSON JONES**

# STORIES ARE NOT WEAPONS

# Stories Are Not Weapons

Bedtime is a time for bonding and building self-esteem, not warfare. If you are tired at the end of the day, and your temper is not always under control, remember that your child is probably feeling the same way. This is a time for extra patience and empathy. Psychologists and other counsellors tell married couples not to go to bed angry. I believe one reason for this is because those emotions will be dwelt upon during sleep in some subconscious way. It is not healthy to be angry or resentful at bedtime. You would be far better off staying up for an extra hour and getting six hours of good sleep instead of seven or eight hours of poor sleep. This advice is about relationships, not just marriage. The same concept applies to your children.

Most children do not have the same degree of self-control as adults have. When you consider that many adults just fly off the handle at a moment's notice, it makes you wonder. When and where did they pick up those habits? It probably started in childhood. We spend about one-third of our lives sleeping. Your brain does not shut off during that time. It's sensible to make those hours productive and not potentially destructive.

Going to bed happy and satisfied has to be better for your health, both physically and mentally.

If you are angry with your children, do not use these stories as a way of getting even with them. Remember, you are the mature adult. Children are not born with knowledge of how to behave. They learn from you. If there is a problem or challenge, can you guess who needs to take responsibility? Yes, it's you. You need to train and explain. I know that sometimes our children can really push our buttons and we have a huge desire to punish them. We feel disappointed and betrayed. We give them so much and still we do not get co-operation. The word 'frustration' only begins to describe how we sometimes feel. Just remember that you probably made a choice to have a child, or at least keep the child. I know that when you pictured your future child, they were well behaved at all times and a constant source of pride and joy. So now reality has set in and, just like with most relationships, there are bumps along the way. Welcome to the world of being a parent! Every day is a test. No, every day is a final exam. If you were not as well prepared for today as you had hoped, do not take it out on your child. Telling these stories together is designed to heal and bond. Never use bedtime stories to exact revenge or to punish. They are too useful for providing valuable life-lessons and greasing the wheels of life for the next day.

Holding on to anger is like grasping a hot coal with the intent of throwing it at someone else; you are the one getting burned.

**BUDDHA**

# THE POWER
## OF WORDS

# The Power of Words

Your own words are the bricks and mortar of the dreams you want to realize. Your words are the greatest power you have. The words you choose and use establish the life you experience.

**SONIA CHOQUETTE**

## Empowering Words

Here is a list of words and phrases that empower. They are words that build confidence and give us the ability to follow through on what we must do. Actions come from thoughts. Thoughts come from words. The better our words are, the better our actions will be. The better our actions are, the better our lives will be.

## WORDS AND PHRASES THAT EMPOWER

I am.

I can.

I can do this.

I am sure.

I am certain.

I am confident.

We will succeed.

I know.

Yes.

Thank you.

Great job.

Good work.

Great attitude.

How can I do this better?

How can I learn from this situation?

How can I improve my results in _____?

How can I be a better friend?

How can I be an excellent student?

How can I energize myself today?

How can I excel in my favourite sport?

You can have your characters ask empowering questions when everything is falling apart in their little world. Here are some examples:

'How can we save Splashy from the crocodile?'

'What can we do to be better superheroes?'

'How can we get to the Ladder Planet in the next 10 minutes?'

'How can I best use my super powers to win against the Spinning Attack Turtle?'

Empowering questions start us thinking about answers. Disempowering questions cause us to wallow in self-pity and inaction. Actions we take and thoughts we think create patterns. Help your child to get into the habit of empowering themselves in any situation. Whatever we focus on is where our time and energy go. Asking questions that move us towards solutions makes us resourceful and powerful.

Your characters can also ask questions that prevent future problems. Examples:

'How can we make sure that the giant crazed crickets can never tear up the tracks again?'

'What can we do now to keep the water from leaking into the submarine?'

'How can we get enough Magic Dust so Tooty can fly all the way around the world next week?'

## WORDS AND PHRASES THAT CAN DISEMPOWER

*I'll try* – means doing without succeeding. 'I'll try to do better,' as opposed to, 'I'm fully committed to exceeding expectations.'

Empowering words to use instead:
**'I will find a way to succeed.'**

*I hope I can* – not the kind of 'hope for a better world'. It's the kind like, 'I hope I pass the test.' That means you would *like* to but you do not believe you will. The only reason for not believing it is lack of experience and preparation.

Empowering words:
**'I will.'**

*I think* – as in, 'I think the plan will work.' As opposed to, 'I have confidence that the plan will succeed.'

Empowering words:
**'I will,' 'I know I can.'**

*But* – this word negates whatever comes before it. 'I think your idea is great, but...' Whatever is coming next will show that the idea is not great.

Empowering words:
**'and ...'**

*Never* – few things are likely to never happen, especially when we are referring to human achievement.

Empowering words:
**'It's not likely,' 'It could happen.'**

*That's impossible* – these words have been proven inaccurate so many times throughout history it's not funny any more. Remember the *Titanic*. They also used to say that man would never fly.

Empowering words:
**'That could happen.'**

*I'm stupid* – while many people do not think as clearly as they might, labels can often stick in the subconscious mind. Do not call people stupid, especially yourself. Ideas can be stupid; not people.

Empowering words:
**'If I work at it, I can learn anything.'**

*I doubt it* – doubt kills confidence. It's better to say, 'I will reserve judgement on that.' Such a strategy leaves more doors open.

Empowering words:
**'There are always possibilities.'**

*What's wrong with me?* – this presupposes an internal lack or problem that may not exist. Try 'How can this situation be resolved?'

Empowering words:
**'How can I do better?'**

*Why can't I do this?* – don't focus on why you can't. Seek ways in which you can.

Empowering words:
**'How can I learn to do this?'**

*Why can't I ever understand _____?* – this assumes you will never understand. With enough time and effort, anything is understandable.

Empowering words:
**'What can I do to get this?'**

*I'll never be a _____!* (profession or performer, sports position)

Empowering words:
**'What can I start doing today to become a _____?'**

*I can't* – it doesn't get much worse than this one. We're defeated before we begin.

Empowering words:
**'I can.' Success comes in cans!**

*I'm stuck* – you haven't worked at it hard enough or tried coming at the problem from a different perspective.

Empowering words:
**'I can get out of this.'**

*This never works for me* – affirming this keeps us from finding solutions. We find creative ways for things to not work out.

Empowering words:
**'I can find a way to do this.'**

Whether you think you can do a thing or think you can't, you're probably right.

**HENRY FORD**

Asking disempowering questions can plague a person for the rest of their life. It gets them focusing on the problem instead of the solution. They go through life continually finding new ways to get into the same problem, over and over again. In your stories you can illustrate this instantly. 'And so Grumbly Bear continued to wonder why the honey bees always chased him away. For the rest of his life they never shared their honey with him. But Smiley Bear looked for ways to protect the hive, and the bees always made extra honey so Smiley Bear could have his weekly treat.' This illustrates to your child that 'people' who moan and complain continue to have something to complain about. It also shows that people who help others often may be rewarded for their efforts.

## Vocabulary

From time to time I would use words in my stories that were beyond my children's experience. I would interject a word or phrase they had never heard before. That gave us an opportunity to learn new words. Sometimes when I did this I would ask them to guess what they thought the word meant from the context. On occasion they could figure it out, or at least get very close. Then I would praise their efforts and add any other meanings to give them the big picture of what the word meant. The next day I would try to remember to ask them again what the new word was. Sometimes they would remember and sometimes they wouldn't. I would remind them of the word and see if they remembered the meaning. Usually they were interested. From time to time they didn't care. It was important to me because I once learned that our ability to think is partially related to the level or quality of the words we know. It's certainly true about our ability to communicate.

From time to time I would take a look at the vocabulary words they were learning at school that week. I would try to weave one or more of the words into the story. In fact, on more than one occasion their vocabulary words gave me an idea or two about a story line. One of the words was 'condensation'. It triggered an idea about Tooty the Train's supply of Magic Dust getting damp and not working at a critical time. This technique straddles the line between stories and helping children with their homework. Using new vocabulary words in this way helps to seal them in children's (and your!) memory.

# MORALS AND LESSONS

# Morals and Lessons

*Experience is a hard teacher because she gives the test first, the lesson afterward.*

**AUTHOR UNKNOWN**

The way your characters act and interact can teach your children valuable lessons about life. My suggestion is to not 'hit them over the head' with the lessons. Make your lessons subtle. Most of the characters should be good role models for your children. You can also have other personalities that do not always behave well. If you do, make sure they suffer the consequences of their behaviour.

Your children can learn by example from your stories. I believe that the decisions we make help determine the course of our lives. We make hundreds and hundreds of decisions all day long. Some of them have little effect on our future. However, the way we make decisions has a huge effect. These fun stories can be embedded with decisions your characters make which can, excuse the pun, build character. Like everyone else, your children will make plenty of mistakes and poor decisions along the way. By providing them with various examples, you can guide them to making fewer mistakes of great consequence. To be human is to make mistakes.

> Learn from the mistakes of others – you can never live long enough to make them all yourself.
>
> **JOHN LUTHER**

The person who makes no mistakes takes no risks at all. And that is perhaps the biggest mistake of all. Then of course there are some bad decisions (like choosing to take illegal drugs) that are hard to recover from. If we can get our children to understand the consequences of certain kinds of decisions, we can provide them with the framework to live a happier life. The idea is to embody the concepts that help us make the kind of decisions that allow us to grow without doing irreversible damage.

> An expert is a man who has made all the mistakes which can be made in a very narrow field.
>
> **NIELS BOHR**

What you do *not* want to pass on to your children are your fears. Through your characters, you can be brave and clever. Your characters can act with intelligence and caring. They can provide examples that might be difficult for you to provide in your everyday life. Your characters can show the kind of courage and integrity we can all aspire to. So, mixed in among the mayhem and silliness, you can drop little hints on how to lead a more fulfilling life. It does not have to be in everything the characters do, and not in every story. It might be only once a week or so. Perhaps you might wait until your children are really involved in the stories. That is up to you.

As I've mentioned, one source for my stories was current events. I would have our characters run for president or prime minister, compete in the Olympics, break land-speed records, explore other planets, take a hot-air balloon trip around the world and do anything else I found intriguing in the news. I avoided the nasty news about killings, war and anything else inappropriate for young minds at bedtime. If there was something only mildly controversial, we would deal with it in a humorous way. We would sometimes talk about it the next day. The bedtime story made an easy segue into whatever I wanted them to know about a given topic. Those conversations invited lively discussions about hundreds of topics that allowed me to tell the children about politics, religion, corporate life, education, charity and much more.

'Now you can see why Sarah Seal was so loved by all the other seals. She always saved part of her meal for the baby seals who had no parents. Helping others is usually rewarded in some way. Although she just did it out of the kindness of her heart, without thought of reward, the other seals always got together to protect her from the killer whales.'

He has not learned the first lesson of life who does not every day surmount a fear.

**RALPH WALDO EMERSON**

# CONVERSATIONS
# THE NEXT DAY

# Conversations the Next Day

The next day is a great opportunity to tie up loose ends and explore ideas and knowledge. On the way to school in the car we would sometimes discuss the story from the night before. It was a great way to point out the difference between fantasy and reality. It was also a great time to bring up related topics and get the kids curious about them. I would share what I knew and then both children could benefit from each other's story as well.

All things are possible until they are proved impossible – and even the impossible may only be so, as of now.

**PEARL S. BUCK**

We could often learn from one another, as the children would share things they'd learned in school. Our discussions would also usually provide fuel for that night's story. They would say something like, 'Ooh! Tonight let's have Hampy be a physics professor!' Or she could be whatever we were talking about: a cobbler, an engineer or a sports star. It didn't matter. Whatever got them excited would work. This way we continued the co-operative creativity into the next day. Sometimes each of the children would come up with an idea from our 'drive time', which meant they would get separate stories. On occasion one of them would be intrigued by the other's idea as well, and they would share both stories. The important thing was that I did not have to do all the 'work'. They provided plenty of great ideas, which we looked forward to for that night or future ones.

Sometimes I would give them hints during the day as to what might transpire that evening. Little teasers would pique their interest and motivate them when bedtime came along. They knew I had something in mind and couldn't wait to find out what it was. They might be discussing a topic at the dinner table and I would casually add that Hampy might have something to say about that later. When they were really young I could sometimes catch a little sparkle in their eye. As they got older they might roll their eyes, trying not to appear too eager about the possibilities. However, as we were about to begin they would ask if Hampy was indeed going to be dealing with whatever I mentioned earlier. So even when they wanted to be cool about it, I knew they had been thinking about it, or at the least hadn't forgotten about it altogether!

Another fun element to add is *themes*. You can decide that all the stories for a week (or whatever length of time you desire) will follow a particular theme, unknown to the children. It is up to them to guess the theme. You can even keep a theme going until they guess it. You can have a prize for whoever guesses it first. Of course, if their ages vary a lot you may need to compensate for the youngest. The prize can be that the winner gets to pick the next theme. That new theme can either be announced, or the other children can try to guess it.

Some themes can be easy to guess, others can be rather elusive. Here are some examples of possible themes you can use: the future, cars, food, school, music, weather, birds, the past, brothers, sisters, perspective, forgetting, friendship, birthdays, getting lost, discovery, string, television, performing, playing games, shapes, colours, paper, sound, maths, texture, numbers, pets, animals, plants – the list is fairly endless.

I would suggest not doing themes until you've thoroughly established your bedtime routine. It's something to add later to add interest and another level. You may want to consider only one guess per night. If they are making endless guesses it can get a bit time-consuming (not to say annoying!). They could be given two guesses, or whatever number you feel would be appropriate for your children. My reasoning for limiting their guesses is so they have the opportunity to really think through their guesses. They must think clearly and learn to prioritize their choices. You can also use their wrong guesses for themes and ideas later on!

# GOAL-SETTING

# Goal-setting

When we are motivated by goals that have deep
meaning, by dreams that need completion, by pure
love that needs expressing, then we truly live life.

**GREG ANDERSON**

You can use your bedtime stories to introduce your children
to the concept of goal-setting. Let's cover the basics. Somebody once said that a dream is not a goal until it is written
down. A goal is a well-defined end point that you are actively
engaged in achieving. The concept is so simple that most
people overlook it. And yet it is one of the most powerful
tools anyone can have in their quest for a better life.

A problem clearly stated is a problem half solved.

**DOROTHEA BRANDE**

Defining where you are going sends you along that path.
An example would be going out for dinner. One way to

proceed is to get in the car and just start driving around until something looks appealing. A better way is for someone to say, 'Let's go to Mama's Pizza Shack.' Now the goal is defined and clear to everyone. You know the way, or can call for directions, or go to their website, or use a SatNav device. Once the goal is clear, a variety of means to the end pop into your brain. This is one value of goal-setting.

If you like pizza, there is another value: motivation. Having a clearly defined goal can provide the motivation to keep taking action until you achieve it. Vague, fuzzy notions do not inspire us to take action. If you do research, you will find something called SMART goals. Those letters stand for Specific, Measurable, Attainable, Realistic and Tangible. I would add 'IM' to the beginning. The 'I' stands for Image and the 'M' stands for Motivating. Now you end up with goals that say 'I'M SMART.' Hey, that would make a great registration plate!

The only one to watch out for is the R. Most people set their standards for 'realistic' far too low. You will never know how much you are capable of until you set your goals higher than you think you can achieve. My clients always outperform what they thought was realistic. Just don't set your goals so high that you can't believe in them. Use the 'realistic' part for setting your goals higher than you would normally do.

You cannot use the same rule when setting goals for others, however. With children, start with goals they feel they can achieve. First arrive at a mutually agreeable goal, following their lead. Unless what they set is ridiculously low, go with it. They have a whole lifetime to set higher goals. Let them first learn through making their own decisions. Later the child can change the set point higher if they want the added challenge.

You don't have to be a fantastic hero to do certain
things – to compete. You can be just an ordinary chap,
sufficiently motivated to reach challenging goals.

**SIR EDMUND HILLARY**

You can gently introduce children to the idea of goal-setting
by having one or more of your characters use this technique.
Of course, if your child is very young (three to six years old or
so), you want to keep it very simple. The character will probably
not be taking out a notebook and writing down measurable
goals. They will say something simple like, 'OK, Mr Worm,
our goal is to get that weed out of the garden.' Mr Worm could
ask, 'When you say "out of the garden," does that mean it has
to go past the fence?' You have just introduced your child to
the concept of clarity and defining a goal. You don't have to
make a big deal of it. If you have a few of those in your stories
every week, your child will get the idea. Soon you may see
them displaying that kind of clear thinking in everyday life.
'So, Mum, when you say "take the rubbish out," do you mean
all the way to the bin, or just outside the door?' OK, so that
was a bit cheeky, but you get the idea.

One of the most important things we can teach our children
is how to communicate clearly. Clear communication is one
of the keys to getting what we want and need. Having your
characters clearly communicate well-defined goals teaches
both concepts at once.

The most powerful way to set a goal is to create a mental
picture of the goal achieved. For example, say that you want
a new car. The first step is to decide which model you want.
Now you have part of the picture in your head. What you
need next is to put *yourself* in the picture. See yourself sitting

behind the wheel. That's pretty good, but we can do better. It would be more motivating to *see yourself driving where it would excite you the most. Imagine yourself zipping along the coast road, wind in your hair, your favourite music blasting through the speakers. You feel the wheel in your hands and reach over to touch the luxurious seats. You admire the wood-grain dashboard console and sense the tyres gripping the road on the tight turns.* Now, isn't that better than 'I suppose I need to get another car'? Which is more fun and motivating? Of course, your visualization will be suited specifically to your lifestyle. Perhaps you are driving blissfully down the motorway while the children watch a DVD on the drop-down monitor. Whatever floats your boat is what you use to paint your canvas. The same is true for your stories. Have your characters show vision. One could say, 'I see us sitting on a beach under a big blue umbrella, sipping pineapple juice and watching the waves splash on the rocks.' By describing the picture in your head, other people know what you want. Until we paint such mental pictures in class, most of my clients don't really know specifically what they want. Putting our dreams into vivid pictures helps us realize what they are. I call this concept 'End-of-the-Movie'. It's just like the last scene in the old Westerns. The cowboy rides off into the sunset. If he is able to do that, then all the problems he faced in the story must have been overcome (the horse throwing a shoe, the shoot-out, the cave-in, etc.). You can do the same thing with your own End-of-the-Movie for any project you undertake. That includes one for telling your story. Before you begin, *see* your child thanking you and hugging you at the end as you say good night.

Helping your children put their dreams into clear mental pictures will help them achieve more in life. Remember, dreams are only dreams until they are written down.

And they become powerful when they are written down in the form of pictures with you in them.

The final element is emotion. You need to define how you want to feel in the picture. You need to say it to yourself and feel it. 'I'm thrilled to be in my new car.' 'I feel powerful and feel pride of ownership.' Your brain understands emotions. Your brain likes those feelings, too. It will work harder to get you to the place where you'll feel those emotions. Your characters can do this as well: 'It will feel great to finally have that weed out beyond the fence!' Children like emotions and feelings. They want their characters to be multi-dimensional. Giving your characters feelings helps bring them to life. You can either have the characters put these things into words or you can, as narrator, state them yourself: 'Mr Worm felt great as he stood there seeing the weed on the other side of the fence.'

To sum it all up, setting goals moves us towards them, and often brings our goals closer to us. The clearer we are, the more likely it is we'll get there. The more motivating goals are, the more likely it is that we will put in the energy needed. Making them measurable lets us know how far we have to go. Putting them into pictures brings it all together in a format our brain understands best. Remember the lesson with Big Ben? Pictures are more powerful than words. Pictures take priority in your brain. Remember the saying, 'A picture is worth a thousand words.'

Concentrate on finding your goal,
then concentrate on reaching it.

**COLONEL MICHAEL FRIEDMAN**

# WHEN YOU'VE AN AUDIENCE OF MORE THAN ONE

# When You've an Audience of More than One

If you have more than one child of appropriate age, the question arises of how many times you tell a story in one evening. Do you tell stories to each individual child? Do you tell one story for all to hear at once? Or do you group children according to age, development or interest? If there are separate stories, do you tell the same one with variations for each child, or exactly the same story but to one child at a time? The answer is: it depends!

A number of factors will decide the answer, and it may well change over time. I want you to be aware of the possibilities, because your children will certainly be aware of how they want things. Let's take these things one at a time.

## Two Children
Your choices are fairly simple here. You can either tell them together or one at a time. Let's examine the benefits and drawbacks for telling both at the same time.

### Benefits
It saves you time.

The children get to sleep sooner.

You only need to come up with one story – no variations.

### Drawbacks
One child will need to get out of bed and into their own when the story's over.

They may argue over whose room the story gets told in.

Neither child gets one-to-one attention.

They may fight or annoy one another.

One may be more sophisticated, leading to boredom for one or feelings of inadequacy in the other.

If you tell them stories separately, you may need to come up with a completely different story for each. While that can be more fun, if you are overtired or feeling ill it can seem like hard work. However, I can tell you that there were many times when I felt poorly and telling a story perked me up. I had far more energy afterwards. Sometimes when our expectations are low we relax more and out pops a truly inspired idea. Oftentimes genius strikes when we get out of our own way. Some of us tend to overthink things or we are too critical of ourselves. When we let go, for whatever reason, the outcome can often be well above average.

A lot of this depends on your children's ages and when you start the storytelling tradition. Let's say you start with a 4-year-old. You've been telling the stories for a year and a new baby comes along. By the time your second child is old enough for such stories, you have a well-developed pattern with your oldest. There will come a day when you decide that the younger child should get his or her own stories. Either the child will ask or you will not want to water down the stories for the older child. Once the decision is made, that's pretty much the way it will be.

Exceptions are when you are driving at night and both children are together and there is no way to separate them for the stories. You can still tell two separate stories. They just hear both. That happened fairly often with us, since both children liked different things to happen. Often my oldest would point out things that would not work in his sister's story. Since those things did not bother her for a long time, I would ask him to keep his observations to himself until later. Not only did she not care about those discrepancies, she did not want him disturbing the flow of the story. It came down to the level of sophistication for their ages and their concern over what was possible or not. This is why I mentioned using different versions of the same plot for different children. It's like the old saying, 'Different strokes for different folks.'

## Three Children

Things can become delightfully complex after two children. At this point, you can begin to think about groupings instead of individual one-to-one sessions. One-to-one is fine if you have the time and energy. A lot depends on the ages of the children. If they are separated by more than three years, their bedtimes may be far enough apart to warrant each getting their own story. Or it's possible an older child might want to hear their story with a younger sibling, and then go off to bed later. Remember, one of the reasons for these stories is to wrap up the day and BE in bed at the conclusion of the story. All your children will have different personalities and they may go back and forth on what they desire. Your job is to co-ordinate that with flexibility and patience, tempered by time frames and your family's version of reality.

The whole thing may come down to bathroom logistics. If you have a limited number of bathrooms, you may simply have to stagger the stories anyway. The youngest child gets cleaned up and watered, and then gets their story. At that moment, the next oldest starts washing, and so on. It's the assembly-line approach. If they cannot all get washed up at about the same time, there's not much choice. I'm a firm believer in real bedtimes for young children. I can't say we always adhered to it, but I can report that when our children got adequate sleep their behaviour was far better, and we all got along better. The excuse of 'But I'm not tired' is illusory at best. It's true that they may not feel tired at bedtime. Unfortunately, they will feel tired the next day if they do not spend enough horizontal time in bed. It's been said that wisdom is knowing the consequences of your actions. It is wise to go to bed and get the hours required whether or not we feel tired at that moment. In speaking with other parents I get the impression that some children are unaware of how tired they are until it's too late – literally. By the time they are aware of their body's signals, they are overtired.

Be aware that your children may compare notes the next day. I'm not saying this should cause concern. If you give more detail or take one story further, it will be for at least two reasons. One, the second child is older or further developed and can handle more sophisticated concepts. Two, as you tell the story a second time you may get a better idea and include extra bits. When this would happen with my family I'd simply explain that sometimes that's what happens. I usually shared the better idea the next day anyway.

Better is the enemy of good.

**VOLTAIRE**

# When Friends or Relations Stay over

To find a friend one must close
one eye – to keep him, two.

**NORMAN DOUGLAS**

The stories and characters you develop may become very personal. You may have many in-jokes and understandings that would be hard to explain to an 'outsider'. Your characters are a combination of personal likes and dislikes that develop over time in private moments. The choice of revealing these to other people should be discussed *before* a friend or relative stays over or you stay over at their home. One reason is that someone new to it could use the characters or the storytelling itself as something to tease your child about. There may be some friends they want to share your stories with and some they will not. It could embarrass the other child by suggesting inviting them when they are standing there. Once you bring it up, it would be rude not to include them. So sharing stories should be discussed thoroughly *before* your guest arrives.

I believe a prudent solution is to invite the child to share in the story, explaining that you have favourite characters you have adventures with. They are welcome to listen along with your child. You then have a second choice. You should definitely decide ahead of time whether the visiting child can make suggestions to the story. While they may get excited and wish to be more involved, be prepared to deal with

171

suggestions that may be totally counter to your characters' personalities. Using Elmo as an example, you probably know at least one child who would suggest that Elmo beat up another character, or worse. Assuming you view that as wrong, you need to deal with it without psychologically harming the visiting child. I would suggest enlightening the child by explaining that in these stories, Elmo would not behave that way. If they disagree, tell them they are free to create any story they wish in their head or at their home, but in your home this is the way you do it. Later, without much delay, you might discuss this with your child, pointing out the difference between the way you do things and the way this child is being raised. You can explain why you believe it's important. I also recommend doing this without passing judgement on the other child or their family. They are (most probably) not evil, just different. As you know, you may establish any guiding moral principles you wish in your home. You are not obliged to put up with interference from outside sources. All you are obliged to do is not lower the self-esteem of visitors to your home. This may be like walking a fence, but that's life.

The other solution is to tell your story in private, possibly away from the bedroom if the visiting child is sleeping in the same room. Simply announce that you need to speak to your child about a family matter, and wish the visiting child good night. Tell them that your child will return in a few minutes. If they ask what it's about, just gently repeat that it's family business. Saying it with a friendly tone of finality should end the discussion. 'It's just *family* business, *you* know.' The '*you* know' part will (gently) pressurize them into not wanting to reveal that they have no idea what you are on about. Coach your child to respond the same way when they return, if asked. Then they should change the subject to a game they played earlier or tomorrow's events. For example, 'Which ride do you want to go on first at the funfair?' That should provide enough distraction. If not, suggest they try, 'I'm really tired. I want to get enough sleep for tomorrow.'

The important thing to consider is protecting the integrity of what you are doing. If it means keeping certain things private, so be it. Sometimes we cannot share all things with all people. In our case, my children told their friends about our stories with pride and their friends were very curious to hear the stories for themselves, so I was happy to share with them. We did not experience any problems with it. In fact, I think some of the children were a bit envious that we were close enough to share such (often very silly) adventures together. I believe they wished their parents would do the same for them. In part, that's why I have written this book. We have had children over to our home who were amazed that our family sat down together to share a meal, all at the same table. I'll grant you that we could not pull that off every day once outside activities took precedence, but we made the effort and achieved it a lot. We sort of took it for granted, while other children thought it was only something that happened on reruns of TV programmes from the 1970s. In a similar way, visiting children were often astonished that my children's dad spent this time with them making up wonderful daft stories every night. I want to help you to be that daft dad (or mum!).

> You may be disappointed if you fail, but you are doomed if you never try.
>
> **BEVERLY SILLS**

# TELLING STORIES
# LONG-DISTANCE

# Telling Stories
# Long-distance

The only trick here is the logistics of having them in bed, all washed up. Since you are not physically there, someone else must be responsible for seeing to it that they are properly prepared for bed. If I was out, I would call ahead of time to give ample notice of when I'd be available to tell a story. If they were almost ready I would just hang on. If they were not, they would either call me back or I would call back at a specific time.

If your children are being looked after by the babysitter one night, he or she needs to make sure the children are ready according to any rules you've all agreed. If I were going to be out, I would usually give my kids an extra kiss, telling them that was for later when I told them their story. As far as babysitters go, I'd also suggest writing out some of your rules and routines so there is no confusion or 'playing' the babysitter. You can sign the sheet and even have your children sign as well, like it's a contract. Sometimes it's never too young to start taking responsibility for our agreements.

Be sure you have an exit strategy for hanging up. Have the child call the babysitter at the end. Before they hand over the phone, remind them of the kiss, make the kissy sound, and tell them you love them. End with something like, 'I'd like to speak with (babysitter's name) for a moment. Sweet dreams and good night.' Now they will do one of two things. One, they will hand the phone over. Two, they will ask a question or make a comment. One reason is to stall, in which case just answer quickly or say you'll have to think about it and give them an answer tomorrow. Say good night again and ask for the babysitter. If you have a cordless phone, the sitter can blow the child a kiss and walk out, hanging up later. Or they can hang up there, and the child knows for sure that there is no more easy opportunity to ask for you. Sometimes the firm knowledge that the conversation is over is best.

# KEEPING TRACK OF YOUR STORIES

# Keeping Track of
# Your Stories

If I could do anything differently, I would have kept a record of the stories I've told. I've told thousands, and I cannot remember most of them. Recording the simplest key words in a log-book would have saved me untold hours writing this book, for a start! But not only that – my children and I would have been able to reminisce for hours looking them over. Please take my advice to heart. Keep a simple record of your stories. Here's an example:

*14/8/07 – Told a Tooty. Agra and Vagra came, needed him to solve a problem. All the tracks were vanishing on their planet. They ended up in an underground tunnel system. It belonged to a great ruler – turned out to be Hampy. Hampy rebuilt their tracks later that afternoon – she invented a machine that could do it very fast. Arielle guessed it was Hampy as soon as I said there was a great ruler.*

This gives the date, the characters, the plot and the ending. Equally important, it included my daughter's reaction.

Someday, that could be the best part of the record. You can also use your log for new ideas, playing on an old story. If you have a record like this, you can adapt old stories years later (your children will most likely have forgotten!), revisiting them and making them more sophisticated for your now older children. Even though they may not recall all you have done, if your children look over your log some day in the future, they will appreciate your efforts.

> You must write down all the thoughts and ideas that come into your mind, or they will cease to come into your mind.
>
> **VIRGINIA WOOLF**

# FINAL THOUGHTS

Final Thoughts

# Final Thoughts

Aside from holidays, I think some of the best memories we have as a family are the bedtime stories we shared. They were fun, and we spent hundreds of hours together, just communicating. It wasn't TV, and it wasn't a board game, and it wasn't even a book of other people's thoughts and ideas. This was truly *our* time, with our thoughts and flights of fancy. No matter what the future brings, those hours spent close together in our mutually created worlds will always be there. While we don't remember every adventure, we know there were tons of them. It was something we counted on, and we did it at every opportunity. I can't think of anything else I would do to replace those times. In a world with enough pressure to go around twice, we cuddled up and had fun inventing worlds where problems were solved by silly superheroes of our own design. We stretched our imaginations, honed our thinking skills, and we did it together. We learned, we laughed, and we had a thousand in-jokes.

So have loads of fun with your child and let the ideas flow. You and your children will always cherish the time you spent creating stories together.

When you dream alone, with your eyes shut, asleep, that dream is an illusion. But when we dream together, sharing the same dream, awake and with our eyes wide open, then that dream becomes reality!

**SOURCE UNKNOWN**

# About the Author

Ronny M. Cole is a corporate trainer and personal life coach.
He has created and delivered a number of programmes,
including:

SuperReading®

The Chrysalis Goal Achievement Programme

Lessen the Stressin'

How to Remember Names

How to Win at Any Sport

How to Remember Numbers

He has also written *Zany Knock-Knocks* (NY: Sterling
Publishing Co, Inc., 1993)

Ron's website is www.alchemy.name.

The following pages are intended for you to record brief notes about your stories. Some day, when your children are grown, they can look back and remember the love you invested in their bedtime. I recommend recording the date, the characters and the basic plot. You may also wish to record any special comments from your child. They are priceless and without these notes most of them will not be remembered.

For example:
9/10/95 Tooty, Hampy, Magic Tunnel, Winnie the Worm. Winnie takes her first ride on a train. Amazed how big the world is.

You can abbreviate:
10/10/95 T, H, MT. T and H go to London in the MT. Everybody knows H, including the Queen. T can't believe it when H is knighted! Joseph learned about knights in school. He told me all about it.

Depending on the age of your children and for how many years you tell these bedtime stories, the total amount will likely add up to thousands. There is not enough room on these pages to record them all. I suggest recording the first ten or so and then notes on new characters and those times when you create really amazing gems. I know I created several dozen stories that were spectacular. Most of them are lost to the years (which go far faster than you can believe). So take lots of photos of your family and write down your best creations. If you want to record them all, computers are brilliant for this. However, your best stories, written in your own hand, are a treasure that has no equal.

You will find as you look back upon your life that the moments when you've really lived are the moments when you've done things in a spirit of love.

**UNKNOWN**

_____

_____

_____

_____

_____

_____

_____

_____

_____

_____

_____

_____

_____

_____

_____

_____

Every child is an artist. The problem is how
to remain an artist once we grow up.

**PABLO PICASSO**

_____

_____

_____

_____

_____

_____

_____

_____

_____

_____

_____

_____

_____

Cherish your children for what they are,
not for what you'd like them to be.

**UNKNOWN**

While we try to teach our children all about life,
our children teach us what life is all about.

**ANGELA SCHWINDT**

_____

_____

_____

_____

_____

_____

_____

_____

_____

_____

_____

_____

_____

_____

Imagination is more important than knowledge.
Knowledge is limited. Imagination encircles the world.

**ALBERT EINSTEIN**

The function of the imagination is not to make strange things settled, so much as to make settled things strange.

**G.K. CHESTERTON,** essayist and novelist (1874–1936)

_____

_____

_____

_____

_____

_____

_____

_____

_____

_____

_____

_____

_____

_____

_____

_____

All the beautiful sentiments in the world
weigh less than a single lovely action.

**JAMES RUSSELL LOWELL**

Just don't give up trying to do what you really
want to do. Where there is love and inspiration,
I don't think you can go wrong.

**ELLA FITZGERALD**

## Titles of Related Interest

YOU CAN HEAL YOUR LIFE, the movie,
starring Louise L Hay & Friends
(available as a 1-DVD set and an expanded 2-DVD set)
Watch the trailer at www.LouiseHayMovie.com

THE SHIFT, the movie,
starring Dr Wayne W Dyer
(available as a 1-DVD set and an expanded 2-DVD set)
Watch the trailer at www.DyerMovie.com

\*\*\*\*

*Time management for Manic Mums,* by Allison Mitchell

*How to Stop Your Kids Watching Too Much TV,*
by Teresa Orange and Louise O'Flynn

*The Adventures of Lulu,* by Louise L. Hay

*How to be a Great Single Dad,* by Theo Theobald

*Unstoppable Me,* by Wayne Dyer and Kristina Tracy

*Thank You, Angels,* by Doreen Virtue and Kristina Tracy

We hope you enjoyed this Hay House book.
If you would like to receive a free catalogue featuring additional
Hay House books and products, or if you would like information
about the Hay Foundation, please contact:

Hay House UK Ltd
292B Kensal Road • London W10 5BE
Tel: (44) 20 8962 1230; Fax: (44) 20 8962 1239
www.hayhouse.co.uk

\*\*\*

**Published and distributed in the United States of America by:**
Hay House, Inc. • PO Box 5100 • Carlsbad, CA 92018-5100
Tel: (1) 760 431 7695 or (1) 800 654 5126;
Fax: (1) 760 431 6948 or (1) 800 650 5115
www.hayhouse.com

\*\*\*

**Published and distributed in Australia by:**
Hay House Australia Ltd • 18/36 Ralph Street • Alexandria, NSW 2015
Tel: (61) 2 9669 4299, Fax: (61) 2 9669 4144
www.hayhouse.com.au

\*\*\*

**Published and distributed in the Republic of South Africa by:**
Hay House SA (Pty) Ltd • PO Box 990 • Witkoppen 2068
Tel/Fax: (27) 11 467 8904
www.hayhouse.co.za

\*\*\*

**Published and distributed in India by:**
Hay House Publishers India • Muskaan Complex • Plot No.3
B-2• Vasant Kunj • New Delhi - 110 070
Tel: (91) 11 41761620; Fax: (91) 11 41761630
www.hayhouse.co.in

\*\*\*

**Distributed in Canada by:**
Raincoast • 9050 Shaughnessy St • Vancouver, BC V6P 6E5
Tel: (1) 604 323 7100
Fax: (1) 604 323 2600

\*\*\*

Sign up via the Hay House UK website to receive the Hay House
online newsletter and stay informed about what's going on with your
favourite authors. You'll receive bimonthly announcements
about discounts and offers, special events, product highlights,
free excerpts, giveaways, and more!
**www.hayhouse.co.uk**

# JOIN THE HAY HOUSE FAMILY

As the leading self-help, mind, body and spirit publisher in the UK, we'd like to welcome you to our family so that you can enjoy all the benefits our website has to offer.

 **EXTRACTS** from a selection of your favourite author titles

 **COMPETITIONS, PRIZES & SPECIAL OFFERS** Win extracts, money off, downloads and so much more

 **LISTEN** to a range of radio interviews and our latest audio publications

 **CELEBRATE YOUR BIRTHDAY** An inspiring gift will be sent your way

 **LATEST NEWS** Keep up with the latest news from and about our authors

 **ATTEND OUR AUTHOR EVENTS** Be the first to hear about our author events

 **iPHONE APPS** Download your favourite app for your iPhone

 **HAY HOUSE INFORMATION** Ask us anything, all enquiries answered

join us online at **www.hayhouse.co.uk**

 292B Kensal Road, London W10 5BE
T: 020 8962 1230 E: info@hayhouse.co.uk